WHY ARE THERE NO TALL GRANDMA'S?

A Guide To Assist You In
Researching Your
Family History

by
Scott B. Chase

Illustrated by
Carol A. Fairchild

Heart of the Lakes Publishing
Interlaken, New York
1990

Library of Congress Cataloging in Publication

Chase, Scott B., 1958–
    Why are there no tall grandma's? [sic] : a guide to assist you in
researching your family history / by Scott B. Chase ; illustrated by
Carol A. Fairchild.
        p.   cm.
    Inludes bibliographical refrences and index.
    1. Genealogy.   2. United   States—Genealogy—Handbooks,
manuals, etc.   I. Title.
FS16.C45   1990   929'.1'072073–dc20   90–4741
ISBN: 1–55787–072–1 (pbk)

Manufactured in the United States of America
ISBN: 1–55787–072–1

A *quality* publication of
Heart of the Lakes Publishing
Interlaken, New York 14847

To my grandfather, Rolfe Baker Chase

ACKNOWLEDGEMENTS

This is to express my appreciation and gratitude to all who helped with this book, including my wife, Cathy, my mother and father, my sister, Kristi, and my good friend Wayne Arnold whose suggestions and comments were invaluable.

To my colleague Scott Gerger and my sister-in-law, Laurie Stuart.

To all of you who have unknowingly assisted and inspired me continuously throughout the creation of this work.

CONTENTS

PREFACE

Genealogy, the study of the descent of a person, is a hobby that practically anyone with a little curiosity about history, their own history, can enjoy. There is no restriction on the age or location of the researcher and certainly no set amount of time that must be spent seeking information. In other words, you research for as long and as often as you wish. You are your own boss and you set your own pace.

When you think about genealogical research consider yourself to be a master detective trying to solve the ultimate mystery. The elements are exactly the same. Who did it? (who is the father?); what was the motive? (what was his occupation?); when did it happen? (when was he born?); where did it happen? (where was he born?); why did it happen? (why did he move west?); and how was it done? (how did he meet mother?). Knowing the answers to these questions about any ancestor will extend the knowledge of your family history further into the past.

The most interesting aspect of this type of detective research is, of course, that the mystery you are solving is about you! You may learn that you are a descendant of royalty, possibly a Mayflower immigrant, perhaps a watch maker, or maybe even a witch who was hung at the Salem witch trials in 1692. Any of these are possible and the following guide will help you to learn exactly which history is yours.

One of the more fortunate things about getting involved in genealogy is the number of people you meet who will assist you with your research. Whether it is a telephone call or a letter, most people associated with genealogical material are more than willing to help you with your questions. They may be restricted by privacy laws, which are different for each state, or swamped with dozens of letters just like yours, but they will help you if they can. This is extremely important because without them the searching would be nearly impossible and hardly worth the effort. I can not adequately thank the hundreds of these people who have assisted me with my research.

The biggest reason why I have continued to pursue my family history is the tremendous amount of pleasure it has given me. The people I have met, the places I have visited and the facts I have learned about my ancestors all have contributed to my enjoyment. This is also part of the reason why I have embarked on the task of writing this book. By following the guidelines outlined in the forthcoming chapters you will be able to share in this pleasure by discovering your own heritage.

INTRODUCTION

Why are there no tall grandmas? Have you ever really thought about it? Actually, neither have I, but let's consider it for just a minute. It is certainly true when you get older that your bones and muscles shrink a small amount because of all the years of gravity pulling down on them. It is also true that when your grandmothers were 20 years old and at their physical maturity, the average height of American men and women was one to two inches less than what it is today. People are just growing bigger today than they were 50 years ago.

But neither of these are the real reason. I believe it is the years and years of carrying a purse that has gradually caused their bodies to shrink. Have you ever seen all the "stuff" they carry in one. Those purses just have to be heavy and after sixty years the effects of carrying them wherever they go are obvious and therefore the title of this book.

Seriously though, let's forget about it and get to the task at hand of researching your family history.

A couple of words need to be said up front to clarify the contents of this handbook. This text is not intended for everyone involved in genealogical research. It is for those who are newcomers to the field, or for the casual searcher who might be looking for a few new methods of how to locate information. The veteran searcher probably won't learn anything new. However, even they may get a chuckle or two from "Mr. G." "Who is *Mr. G?*," you ask. I guess you'll just have to keep reading to find out!

In addition to guiding you as you trace your family roots, I will also simplify your research by giving you some little tricks and research techniques that I have picked up while searching my own family history. This may not sound like much but on more than one occasion it has been a very small fragment of information that has led to the discovery of dozens of ancestors. It is these "breakthroughs" that all genealogists look and hope for as frequently as possible.

You will find the information in this book written for beginners. I am not a professional genealogist, nor do I have 20 years of experience in this fascinating research field. I only "got the bug" a few years ago while attending graduate school. In that short time, and I stress "short" for reasons obvious to those who have been researching for a longer period of time than I have been alive, I have located more than 1000 direct relatives, over 500 of whom are my bloodline ancestors. I have also located information which traces one of my lines back to the year 1050 (that's William The Conqueror's time for you history buffs).

So, why then do I feel that I am qualified to write about this subject? For two very simple reasons. First, the success I have had researching several persons' genealogies, other than my own, has helped me to develop a "cookbook" method of research. This method is very basic and so straightforward that I felt the need to share it. On several occasions people who knew I was researching my family history made the comment, "I would like to do my family history also, but I don't know how to get started." This reason is heard all over quite frequently, and hearing this myself made me consider writing this book.

The second reason, which concerns the lack of clear, helpful published genealogy "How-To" books, convinced me that a guide such as this is desperately needed. Most of the currently available guidebooks of which I am aware (see bibliography), lack what I feel is the most important quality of a "How-To" book; that is, how to do the research itself! Most of them claim to answer this question but in reality do not. I have read and outlined in detail six of the books listed in the bibliography under "How-To," and what I have found is that they answer three other questions. These are "What resources are available to you, the researcher?", "What information do they contain?" and "How do you make use of these resources?" These are, of course, extremely important questions to answer, but they are not complete in themselves. The key is knowing which of these resources to use for a particular ancestor you are researching. I feel that this is the most important aspect of conducting genealogical research to know how to utilize. How I accomplish this is evident from the format of the book being laid out in specific time periods by chapter.

You will find that the second chapter covers the years from the present to 1910, the third from 1910 to 1790 and so forth. The reason why I have broken the research down in this manner, is that the resources and information that are available to you, the searcher, are vastly different depending upon the century or even half century you are researching. Federal census records don't start until 1790 and if you are trying to locate a family who lived in the 1730s, you will have to resort to something else. Exactly which resources are available for each time period and how to make use of them is outlined in each chapter.

I have probably made this sound simpler than it really is, but consider the following. The information about your ancestry probably can be located if you know how and where to look for it. However, yes here it comes, there are certain criteria which would be to your benefit and which you have absolutely no control over, that would greatly simplify your research and increase your chances for success. What do I mean by this? If your ancestors have been in the United States for many years, possibly centuries, you are the ideal descendant because they can more than likely be traced. In addition, if any one of your family lines can be traced to an English, Irish, or Scottish immigrant, you may be able to tie into one of the publications known as Burke's Peerage. These are genealogy references that have been published for more than a century in over 100 volumes. These volumes list tens of thousands of family genealogies in startling detail. The key is to connect one of your lines to one that they have published. The probability that you will be successful in making this connection is quite low but they still should be checked.

There are also a large number of books published which give fairly complete histories of the Kings and Queens of Scotland, and the Lords and Deputies of England and Ireland. If you can connect any of your ancestral lines to this royal blood you again have certain advantages. Achieving success with these records is even more remote, but, who knows, you could get lucky.

Now, for those of you who may not be so fortunate, genealogically speaking, consider the following. The first three chapters will be the most useful to you if you, your parents, or your grandparents are the original immigrants to the United States. Unless you can locate information that has been previously researched and published in the US by others from your homeland, you will have to contact that particular homeland directly for the older records you are seeking. As you can probably guess information of this nature is quite scarce but more people are researching it now than ever before.

Another handicap, genealogically speaking, would be if one of your ancestral lines is descended from Native Americans. Their records are, putting it mildly, extremely scarce and tracing your family history through their records would be next to impossible. Doane and Bell provide a fairly complete listing of what records there are concerning Native Americans. Yet another handicap would be if you are descended from black ancestors. Unfortunately most records dated before 1900 containing information on Black Americans are extremely incomplete, if they exist at all. Blockson's "Black Genealogy" gives a fairly complete treatment of this subject. The bottom line for this text is:

> this book will help you locate information about any of your ancestors who was born, married, or died in America, specifically those who were not Native or Black Americans.

Although many of the resources may not exist at all, the research procedures presented in this text can help you a great deal. The time period approach teaches the researcher to break the information gathering process down into smaller brackets of years which are based on when the resources are available. This helps to organize what to do next.

Now, I would like to discuss in more detail the usefulness of the other genealogy "How-To" books which I briefly referred to earlier. What they do offer is information on the types of records available for conducting genealogical research. Depending upon which book you select will determine which of the many resources the author covers in detail. Each author had in his own mind what he or she thought was most important and discussed it fairly extensively. One of the best reference books that discusses most of the available genealogy reference material is *The Source.* I refer to it several times throughout this text.

These books also discuss how to make use of these records. For the most part this is useful, however it is not required. The librarians, city and town clerks and other professional genealogists will assist you in using any of the resources. Once you obtain this initial "how-to-use" knowledge for any resource, you can put this aside and concentrate on finding your ancestors.

A common characteristic of most of these books is their formal nature. Researching your family history should be fun! I find that when there is a little bit of humor "in the air" the researching effort seems to proceed more smoothly and quickly. I have attempted to take a little bit of the scientific rigor, evident in these books, out of my methods while preserving the basic research process. Only you can tell if I am successful or not.

You may ask yourself what goals you should set as your research days go on. Certainly, locating every direct ancestor is the ultimate goal, but there are practical limits as to how far back you can go. For example, if it were not for duplication of people (which I will explain shortly), to locate every direct ancestor back 2000 years to the time of Christ, you would be trying to find a thousand billion billion people, all of whom would be related to you. This is certainly preposterous since it has been estimated that only 75,000,000,000 humans have been born and died in the last 600,000 years. Lucky for us most known family records don't go back much further than William The Conqueror's time (1028 to 1087). Even so, this would be an impossible task with 4,294,967,296 people to locate.

A more realistic goal is to locate all your ancestors back to the original American immigrant. This is quite achievable even if some of your family lines go back to the time of the Pilgrims (1620). This is possible for a few of your family lines but certainly not all because there were only 102 Pilgrims and you could have as many as 1000 ancestors in your tenth generation alone! Even if it were so, you would be trying to locate between 4000 and 8000 people in all. I myself know of 515 direct ancestors, all of whom either immigrated to or were born in America. For those of you interested in where these numbers came from, see the Direct Ancestor Table in the Appendix.

As I mentioned, these numbers are not totally accurate because of duplication of ancestors. By this I mean your great-great-great-great-grandfather could have married one of his distant sixth or seventh cousins. It happens quite frequently without much notice. In fact after three years of research, I learned that my mother and father are ninth cousins twice removed! This means that there is a common ancestor to each side of my parents' lineage. From that ancestor and further back there will only be one pedigree and not two. This duplicate line greatly reduces the total number of my direct ancestors. This is an example of why the numbers in the Direct Ancestry Table are deceptively high.

The most important thing, without a doubt, when doing genealogy research is time and lots of it. This book and all other "How-To" books are useful, of course, but without the time necessary to use them or any other research material, they will not be of much use to you. I don't mean to scare you away but the fact remains that you are searching for information that is one, two and even three hundred years old. I am not saying that this is an impossible task, but persistence, which takes time, will yield good results with your research.

Lastly, a discussion of the validity of researched information is necessary. It is important that you NEVER assume that the information you hear or read is absolutely correct, no matter what the source is. I have not yet found a single source of information, such as personal interviews, federal and state census records, birth, marriage, and death records, wills, etc., that is 100% correct for every person I have researched. You will find most of these records to be accurate, but not all of them. After all, we humans have been known to make mistakes before, and any information you uncover was at one time recorded by fellow brethren. The last thing you want to do is to spend your valuable time following up on erroneous information. The trick is to identify which information is not entirely correct. This can only be accomplished by second and third sources and sometimes by common sense. Only then, will you learn what is true and what is not. The message here is: BE AWARE OF POSSIBLE ERRORS (BAOPE)!

Example #1

To stress this point further let me give you an example. During the course of a telephone interview, I was told that the woman I was researching, the interviewee's paternal grand-mother, was from Port Allegany, PA. In fact, I was told that she remembered seeing her back in the early 1920s when she, herself, was about six years old. Proceeding with this, I checked the available resources. After weeks of turning up absolutely nothing,

I went back to my notes and files and started over on a different path. That is when I found my answer. Part of my original information from the interview was incorrect. Which part? It was the interviewee's maternal grandmother, not paternal, that she had remembered seeing when she was just a child. This means of course a different maiden surname. Locating genealogy material from the correct information went quite well. The message is,

BAOPE!

TOPICS:

vocabulary

genealogy forms

pedigree chart numbering system

family interviews

letter writing

computer genealogy

genealogy scams

GETTING STARTED

No matter what scientific field or topic of discussion is at hand, there are certain "buzz words" that are associated with that particular field. Genealogy is no exception and I thought that it might be useful to list a few common terms with their definitions. I decided to arrange them here instead of in a glossary because some of these terms need more of an explanation than merely a Webster-like definition. The following list is certainly not totally complete. It contains what I feel are the most important terms for the beginning genealogist to know.

Vocabulary

ancestor: one from whom a person is descended: forefather (Webster).

descent: derivation from an ancestor: birth: lineage (Webster).

family group sheet: a listing of all the bloodline family members of a single family and their vital information; father, mother, sons, daughters.

genealogy: from the Greek roots GEN meaning race, kind or birth and LOGY meaning science, study, or account of. Literally defined as "account of a race or family." More popular definition "history of the descent of a person or family from an ancestor or progenitor" (Levine).

pedigree chart: a table listing the ancestral lines or lineage of an individual.

progenitor: an ancestor in the direct line: a biologically ancestral form.

The Appendix contains both blank and completed sample copies of a Family Group Sheet and a Pedigree Chart. You should refer to these often when you are getting started as a guideline for recording your own family information.

There seems to be substantial confusion on three particular

classifications of relatives: higher generation cousins (second and third cousins), someone who is "removed" (Martha is my second cousin twice removed), and someone who is a half brother or half cousin. According to Webster's definition:

> *cousin:* a child of one's uncle or aunt.

This is certainly true, as we all know, but do you know who your second and third cousins are? Your second cousins are your mother's or father's first cousins' kids and your third cousins are . . . Let me suggest some easier definitions:

1st cousin: any person who shares the same grandparent **s** as yourself,

2nd cousin: any person who shares the same great-grandparent **s** as yourself,

3rd cousin: any person who shares the same great-great-grandparent **s** as yourself,

and so forth. You will notice that the "**s**" is in bold type in the word grandparents. The reason is that a full-blooded first cousin must share the same (maternal or paternal) grandmother and grandfather. This leads us to the next two definitions.

half relative: any person who shares only one of your two parents, or grandparents, . . . as yourself.

removed relative: any cousin who is of a different generation as yourself. For example, your father's first cousins are your first cousins once removed.

Finally a few definitions of general interest.

great-relative: a person who is more remotely related by a single generation than a particular direct or sibling relative. For example, your mother's aunt is your great-aunt, your father's grandfather is your great-grand-father.

great-great-relative: a person who is more remotely related by two generations than a particular direct or sibling relative

great-grandbother: the relative who just won't leave after a family picnic!

If you are interested in reading some amazing facts about actual family relationships, such as the woman who learned of the birth of her first great-great-great-great-great-grandson (yes that's five greats!), check out the latest copy of Guinness Book of World Records.

Forms

Before you can start your research you need forms on which to record the vital information about your ancestors. There are two basic types of genealogy forms that serve this purpose well. They are the Pedigree Chart, and the Family Group Sheet which are listed on page 21 in the definitions. As I mentioned, the Appendix contains both a completely filled out and a blank form of each chart for your use.

The Pedigree Chart is capable of recording four generations of peoples' names and associated vital information and a fifth generation of names only. Each fifth generation person is recorded again on a separate form as the "generation number one" person. Sixth through ninth generations are recorded on this form as well and you keep adding forms until you run out of people.

You will need to fill out a separate Family Group Sheet for each and every family you research. Your parents, each aunt/uncle pair, each grandparent pair and so forth, will require a separate form. You can imagine that in a very short period of time you will have gathered quite a large number of Family Group Sheets. Arranging these strictly alphabetically or by family surname might make your filing system more organized.

These two forms are by no means all the possible choices available to you. A copy of the form which I made myself called the Note Taking Form is also in the Appendix. I found that using the standard Family Group Sheet for your permanent records is ideal, but for note taking, letter writing, and quick information gathering purposes, this Note Taking Form works the best for a couple of reasons. When you are conducting personal interviews, you can't be concerned with neatness because it takes too much time. In addition, this form allows for three complete families and their vital information. Any information that you do gather on this form can later be transferred to your original Pedigree Charts and

Family Group Sheets.

Other forms which are available are an 8½×11 version of the Pedigree Chart, Ahnentafel Charts which list the names from the Pedigree Chart, and Descendant Charts which list a single family surname line. Examples of each of these are also given in the Appendix.

I would like to make one final comment about the forms. When you are filling out your original copies you may want to use pencil. The reason for this is that after you have information written on the form you may learn that part of what you have recorded is wrong. If you try to correct ink it could get sloppy and maybe even confusing. You don't want to have to copy the whole chart over if at all possible. Pencil can be easily erased and since you are the only one filling out the forms there is no concern of forgery.

You now have all the necessary tools to get started with your research!

Step #1: Filling In The Pedigree Chart

The first step is to get a copy of the Pedigree Chart and print your full name as given at birth, birth date and birth place in the spaces beneath the labeled "1." Having your own birth certificate in your files is always a good idea. If you do not have this document, contact the vital records department at the clerk's office in the town, village, city, or county in which you were born, and ask the clerk how you can obtain a copy. If you married, put your spouse's full (birth) name, marriage date (and place) in the designated spaces. You will notice that there is no designated space for "place married." I feel that this information is important and should be included on the chart. If you refer to my completed Pedigree Chart in the Appendix you will see how I have included the marriage place.

Step #2: Filling In The Family Group Sheet

Next you need to get a copy of the Family Group Sheet and fill it out for you and your family. If you married, then fill in your name and your spouse's name on the blanks labeled "Husband's Full Name" and "Wife's Full Maiden Name" respectively. Continue filling in the necessary information including any children. If you haven't married, then fill in "Husband's Name" and "Wife's Name" with your father and mother. Continue filling in the form in a similar manner, but here you will be listed in the children's section along with your brothers and sisters. Of course if you did marry then you will need to fill in a chart for both your family and your parents family.

Step #3: Numbering Your Pedigree Charts

For organization, you should adopt a numbering system for your Pedigree Charts. The system I suggest is very simple and allows for indefinite expansion of your charts while maintaining complete order to them. I suggest that your first Pedigree Chart be the chart that lists you and your vital information as person #1. On the space provided on this first Chart, at the upper right hand corner where it says "CHART NO. ____" put an "I" in the blank. The "I" signifies your initial Pedigree Chart.

The next thing you need to do is to fill in all the small blanks which are at the right hand side of the form. Starting with the top blank at the end of the line which is numbered "16," put the number 1. On the line below this one, which is next to the line that is numbered "17," put the number 2 and continue numbering the blanks down to the bottom of the page. Line number "31" will then be numbered 16.

For now you can probably stop numbering charts until you have learned who some of your great-great-grandparents are (the 16 people who will be listed in the columns at the very right of the page). When this happens, and, hopefully, it will, you will have to continue with more charts.

On a blank chart in the upper right hand corner put the number which is to the right of the ancestor you are continuing. This number will be one of the numbers from one to sixteen. On this new chart on the line at the very left which is numbered "1" fill in the ancestor's name and vital information. You now have space for four more generations of ancestors. You will need to follow the same procedure for each of the sixteen people listed in the far right column of your very first chart, chart #I.

Example #2

Let me continue further by using my charts (see Appendix)

as an example. From my very first chart, which is numbered "I", you will find me as the number "1" person. The number "18" person is William Frank Savage and information about him and his ancestry is continued on chart #3. Referring to chart #3 you will see that the people who are numbered from "16" to "31" have chart numbers from 301 to 316. The three representing chart number 3 and the numbers 01 to 16 specifying a particular person on that chart. You then continue numbering all your other charts in a similar manner. This means that Burton Persse, number "31" on chart #I, will be continued on chart #16 and his great-great-grandparents will be continued on charts #1601 through #1616. When it is time to add yet another set of charts to Burton's genealogy, the numbering of them will proceed in the same manner.

By numbering your charts in this manner you can keep track of who the higher generation charts came from. You know that someone on chart #50601 is an ancestor of someone on chart #506. This person in turn is an ancestor of someone on chart #5 who in turn is an ancestor of someone on chart #I. This, of course, takes us right back to you!

Once you have adopted a numbering system, to continue with your research you merely fill in any and all information for each of your parents, then their parents and so forth as shown on the Pedigree Chart. Remember to fill out Family Group Sheets as described previously for each relative pair. "How do you get all this information?" You may want to start with step #4.

Step #4: Family Interviews

Talking to your parents, grandparents, aunts, uncles, etc. is one of the quickest methods of obtaining vital family information. A tape recorder is the ideal "note-taker" because it allows you the freedom to review the information at a later time. It does not slow down the interview as hand writing the information can do. Whatever the method of note taking, the types of questions you should ask of each individual are:

birth date and place   church affiliation
marriage date and place spouse's birth date and place.

When you ask for information about the interviewee's

parents, besides the above questions you should ask:

| mother's maiden name | death dates and places |
| father's occupation | burial places (cemetery, city/town, state). |

Then proceed to ask the same questions about the interviewee's grandparents, aunts, uncles, etc. If the person can't remember something right away, skip it. It might come to them later and, if not, you can probably learn the information from other sources.

This list of questions is by no means complete. You may wish to probe a particular ancestor or relative in more detail. The questions I have listed will obtain the necessary information to extend your family history back one generation at a time. You can see how quickly you can gather a lot of information through interviews.

One thing you have to be very careful of is prying into one of those family "dark areas." Just about everyone has a derelict uncle or a great-aunt who is a "real pill." Since you have absolutely no idea who or what is "not to be talked about" you need to be cautious. If "it" does happen to come up, don't force the issue. There are other ways to obtain the information you are looking for.

When you are conducting an interview, which by the way can certainly be conducted over the telephone (if you don't mind the long distance charges), always try to get as much information as possible. Even if it seems like information about your grandfather's brother, for example, is of little assistance, it may turn out to be just what you are looking for. It has happened with my research on many occasions.

Also you must never forget,

BAOPE.

I defined this in the Introduction as "be aware of possible errors." I have found that most people remember the generalities fairly well, but have a little trouble with the specifics. Some information is apt to be incorrect which makes the challenge for you to identify which part or parts of what they told you is in error.

If you are the oldest living member of your family, then

conducting family interviews may not be appropriate for you. You may have to start your research with the second chapter or possibly with step #5.

Step #5: Letter Writing

This step is probably the most important research tool you will use continuously throughout your researching career. Unless you have the time (and money) to travel to every city or town your ancestors were from, you will need to write letters to the appropriate offices to obtain the information for which you are looking. The following are examples of people and places to which you may need to write letters:

> your own relatives
> cemetery offices
> vital records offices (birth/marriage/death)
> city/town clerks (deeds/tax records)
> surrogate courts (wills)
> churches
> city/town/county historians
> librarians
> historical societies
> private genealogical researchers.

When you are writing relatives, I have found four things which will increase the probability that you will receive a return letter:

1. State why and what you are doing, namely researching your family history as a hobby.
2. Include a stamped self-addressed #10 (long) envelope with your letter. This may sound costly, but compared to traveling or telephone calls it is still the cheapest route.
3. Send a completed Note Taking Form on yourself (and family) as an example for clarity. Also send enough blank Note Taking Forms to cover all the information you are requesting.
4. Ask the person you are writing for addresses of their parents (if applicable), children, etc. This will allow you to write them directly and get more detailed information.

If you are writing a specific records office you need only request the information appropriate for that office. These people are generally very professional and will answer your letters quite promptly if they are not swamped with other requests. Some do request a stamped self-addressed envelope and if you include it with your original letter you might possibly avoid the two or three repeat letters that can result. This is sometimes unavoidable due to the fact that most of these organizations are professional in nature and require their own forms to be completed. They also might require a slight fee for doing the research and for copies before they will assist you.

Letter writing is something that you may end up doing hundreds of times. If you get lucky you may find someone, possibly a great-aunt, who has already gathered some family information. Locating any information at all like this can help you a great deal with your research.

Computer Genealogy

A research tool that is growing in its usefulness to the genealogy researcher is computers and genealogy software. Today there exists several computer programs which help to organize and file any and all of the ancestors and relatives you have discovered. You input the information into the computer and it files the people according to their relationship. You can get a printed copy of any of the charts I have discussed for your files. If you are familiar with computers and are interested in one of these software packages, contact the clerk at the genealogy and local history department of your public library, your nearest genealogy society, or a local computer store (or magazine), to get information about these programs.

One of the biggest advantages I see to these programs is the ease of transferring the information from one floppy disk to another. If you happen to meet someone in your research travels who is a very distant relative of yours, who also has input their information into the computer, you can very easily get copies of each others information by simply making copies of your floppy disks. The rest of us either have to make photocopies or copy everything by hand which can be very time consuming.

I do need to say a few words about the drawbacks to all of

these programs. If you have already gathered a sufficient number of ancestors and associated vital information, in order for you to make use of any of these programs you will have to input every piece of information individually into the computer. This may take a considerable amount of time depending upon how many people you have to input and it may not be worth your while to make this investment. If you are just starting to research your family history, you may want to wait for a time until you have gathered several generations of information. At that time you will be able to make a better judgement as to how deeply involved you wish to get in your research. A more important reason for waiting may be the prospect of what you will learn about your family history. If all of your pedigree lines trace back three generations to the immigrant ancestor, it may not be worth the expense or effort to invest in one of these genealogy programs. You will only learn this by conducting your research.

Genealogy Scams

You may not believe that there could exist people in today's world who would try to take advantage of someone who is trying to research their family history. Unfortunately it is true and I hope that I will be able to help you to recognize the scams that these people offer.

First of all you will very rarely find any genealogist who seeks people out for money rather than for information. Most people who are seriously interested in your family information will contact you directly on an individual basis. Furthermore, they will more than likely be related to you one way or another.

The scams will be presented in a very general manner listing only which surnames they claim to have family genealogy information on. More than likely if you were to pay the $29.95 (or more) they ask, all you will get for your money is a listing of people living around the country that share the same surname as yourself. There probably will not be any mention of how any of them are related if they are related at all. Never succumb to the tempting ads that suggest that for this slight fee you can obtain a copy of your very own family history. You should request specific information about exactly what the person is offering before you pay them anything.

MR. G

TOPICS:

conducting the research

sibling searches

reverse genealogy research

researching distant cousins

complete descendants searches

helpful research tricks

AVAILABLE RESOURCES:

- birth/marriage/death records   IGI
- cemetery records   immigration indices
- church records   • land/mortgage records
- city/town directories   military records
  compiled genealogies   • newspapers
  compiled town histories   ship passenger lists
- family Bibles   • telephone directories
  federal & state censuses   • wills

• denotes the resources discussed in this chapter

TOOLS FOR CONDUCTING THE RESEARCH

current US road atlas

any white pages telephone directory

plenty of notebooks and paper

PRESENT TO 1910

The reference materials which are available to the genealogy researcher for the present day time period, are not as numerous as you might think. Even with modern supercomputers and our high tech society, the availability of useful family information is somewhat limited. I will explain why shortly.

The skills of the present day private investigator are ideal when you are conducting research in this time period. The privacy laws which restrict public access to some of the reference material require the skills of a very resourceful researcher. Some states restrict all access to these records to those who are not registered genealogists. In addition, they may require that the search be conducted by an authorized employee.

For example, in New York State the rules and regulations for obtaining vital records are governed by the Health Commissioner's Office. The information that you get from their offices is of the form of an uncertified copy. An additional restriction is that the search may be conducted only by authorized employees, subject to the following conditions:

1) Information contained on a birth record must have been on file for at least 75 years and the person to whom the record relates is known to be deceased. No information shall be issued from a record that has been placed in a confidential file pursuant to section 4138 of the Public Health Law.

2) Information contained on a marriage record will be issued only from records that have been on file for 50 years or more and the parties named on the record are known to be deceased.

3) Information from a death record will be issued only from records that have been on file for at least 50 years.

If you are looking for vital records for a person who is not a direct blood relative for years after those mentioned above, you may encounter difficulties. You should contact the vital records office of one of the major cities in the state you are interested in, or one of the major genealogy departments, to learn what the rules are for obtaining these types of records for that state. This is NOT a requirement to locate these records, however. You could always try the municipal office directly. They may help you regardless of the formal petitioning of information, because some people just want to help you out.

Those people who are adopted may be well aware of the problems that you encounter when you try to obtain your own birth certificate. The charter of the adoptive agency ALMA, is to assist those people who are either adopted and looking for the identity of their real parents, or are adoptive parents trying to locate their own children. Although they have had over 30,000 successful reunions, there are still more than 750,000 people looking for their blood relations. I will focus my discussions on what I call conventional family research and refer you to these adoptive agencies if you fit this category.

In order to learn what the rules are for your particular state or town, I suggest that you try the following. First, let us assume that you know the town where the person was born, and are looking for their birth record. You should either call or write the clerk's office requesting information about their vital records. "How do you locate the address or telephone number for this office?" This question leads us to the first research trick.

Trick #1

Since you know the town and state where the record is located, get out your white pages telephone directory and find the area code for that town. The area codes for all 50 states and some Canadian Provinces can be found in the very first section of the telephone book labeled "call guide." You should find a map of the United States with every state area code listed on it. The call guide will also list the major cities and their area codes. If you are still not sure where in the state the town is located get out your trusty US Road Atlas and find it. This will help you when you are dealing with states which have several area codes. Now just dial 1-(area code)–555–1212 and ask for the city or town clerk's office for the town of your need. If you do happen to get the wrong area code, the operator will tell you so and inform you as to what the correct one is.

You should try calling the municipal clerk's office during regular Business hours on a weekday. If the records you are looking for are not located at this office, the clerk will inform you so. You should ask where or who has the records and get the address and telephone number.

Once you have located the proper office, you should ask the following questions:

1) What is the procedure for obtaining the information you are looking for.

2) If it seems appropriate, ask the clerk if he/she would check their files for your particular record while you wait.

3) If they will search for you and do locate your record, follow the procedure as described to you by question #1.

You then proceed with a letter or visit to their office according to their instructions. If you get lucky, the clerk might tell you what you want to know over the telephone, and you should be prepared to accept it. This is a quicker way to obtain the information and may be less of a hassle for the clerk.

Doing The Research

This time period (present to 1910) is the one in which most of us start our research. Unless you were born before 1910, you will probably need to make use of the resources discussed in this chapter. Let me try to give some examples of how to do what I just described. The list of resources at the beginning of the chapter is incomplete without a workable procedure on exactly how to locate your ancestors by making use of them.

The goal of your effort for this time period is to learn where and when your parents and grandparents were born and died (if appropriate). Once you learn this, you merely repeat the process over and over until you get back to the original immigrant. The information you are interested in for ANY higher generation ancestor, including your grandparents, is exactly the same as that for your parents; full names, birth, marriage, and death dates and places.

Step #1: Recording your birth date and place on the Pedigree Chart

This step should already have been completed as part of the "Getting Started" stage described in the Introduction. You should refer to that discussion if necessary.

Step #2: Parents' Vital Information

The actual research process starts with your parents and their vital information; this assumes, of course, that you know where and when you, yourself, were born. For a large majority of you, obtaining this information may be as simple as making a telephone call. For others, the information will have to be gathered using the resources listed at the beginning of the chapter.

If your parents are living, you are trying to learn their birth vital information. If your parents are no longer living, you should try to learn their death vital information pursuing cemetery records, death certificates and newspaper obituaries in that order! When you know their death dates and places, then pursue their birth dates and places. "Why is this order so important?" The kind people at the vital records offices prefer an exact date when THEY have to search for the record. If you do not know this date the "I think she was born in November of 1918" statements just won't cut it. You should help these people out as much as possible when you are asking for their assistance.

By starting with cemetery records you may learn all or some of the following information: the person's (your parents) religion, date and place of death, date and place of birth and additional relatives. These records are treated in more detail later.

Once you have located the cemetery records, you should know the death dates of your parents. Now and only now should you search for death certificates and obituaries. The death certificate may be obtained by contacting the department of vital statistics at the municipal clerk's office where the person died. Ask the clerk how you can obtain a copy of the death certificate for your person who died on _____ date. They should be able to assist you from here.

Similarly, an obituary may be obtained by searching through the newspapers local to the town on or shortly after the date the person died. To be sure that newspapers existed for that year, contact the reference department of the main library in the town. If they do exist, then you will either have to go there yourself and search for it, or have someone at the library locate it which usually requires payment of some sort. One of the fortunate things about obituary notices is their complete availability to the general public.

Death certificates and obituaries should inform you as to where and when your parents were born and their parents' names. If this is the case, congratulations, you have successfully completed your first genealogical search! It wasn't that difficult either was it?

For those of you who have been unable to get a copy of your parents death record or the information contained on it, try the following. Check what information is on your own birth certificate. I do not know exactly what information it will contain, but I do know that sometimes they include information about the parents. It may be somewhat dependant upon the year that you were born.

You could also try aunts and uncles if you have any. Sometimes they can tell you one small piece of information that will lead you to new discoveries. A combination of some or all of the above mentioned processes, should result in you learning the birth dates of your parents.

Step #3: Grandparents' Vital Information

At some point in your research, you will locate ancestors whose life spans more than one time period. For example, your grandparents may have been born before 1910 but died several decades later. When this occurs, you will have to use the appropriate chapters for the type of vital information you are searching for. You may have already come across this with your parents if they were born before 1910. If this is the case, then you should use this chapter for determining their death information; the third chapter will aid in determining their birth information.

Obtaining death information about your grandparents is very similar to that described for your parents, with one important difference. You may not have ever known one or more of them when they were alive and you were old enough to remember. Therefore, you may not have any idea where or when they died or are buried. You need to learn this first before seeking their birth and marriage information.

So, what is the very first thing you should do to determine their death dates and places? If you answered personal interviews with your parents, aunts, uncles, great-aunts and uncles and surviving grandparents, give yourself an "A" for outstanding research practice. This is, of course, subject to the condition that any one of these people must still be living. If this is the case, then you should contact them by telephone or letter asking the appropriate questions. Please refer to the discussion on conducting personal interviews in the first chapter for a more complete treatment.

If you are unable to obtain the necessary information through interviews, then you must rely on the resources discussed in this chapter. A good place to start is with the records from the town where each of your parents were born. You should have learned both birth places by successfully completing Step #2.

More than likely, your grandparents were living in the towns where your parents were born the year your parents were born. This means that your grandfathers' names should be listed in the town's city directories or telephone directories, and land and mortgage records. Using the city directories, you should trace each of your grandfathers as far forwards and backwards in time in the directory listings, around the year each of your parents were born.

If your grandparents moved around a lot and didn't die in the towns where your parents' were born, which is very possible, then your work isn't finished yet. You are going to have to keep on searching and I might add that this is where the researching gets tough.

When searching through the directories, you discover that your grandparents disappear. By this I mean, there is no record of them in any cemeteries and there are no death certificates on file. Conclusion, they left town and moved somewhere else, right! Maybe, but not always. It was very common in the early part of this time period, and earlier, to have the elderly parents move in with one of their children. If this did happen it would explain why they just seem to disappear from the city directories. This means that you should find listed other people with the same surname, who you can surmise are related in one way or another to your grandparents. However, if this was the case, then they probably died in that town which means that they should be buried in one of the local cemeteries. This is true unless they were buried in a cemetery in a different location. If neither case is true, then they probably did leave town.

The trick now is to determine where they moved to. Land and mortgage records might help you to determine a more accurate date of their departure. These records can be found at the county clerk's office. Again I refer you to the detailed discussion later in this chapter for a more complete treatment of the use of these records.

Knowing the date of departure more accurately may not seem very important at first but it can help you. For one thing, you know that they didn't die before this date because they were still alive when they moved. This will also help you if you have to search through newspaper articles or other town's city directories. If you only know the departure date to within five years, then you will have to check all five years for every other town you search in to see if they are there. This gets time consuming and tedious very quickly. Always try to get the most accurate date possible when the person you are researching just seems to disappear.

There is one more research technique which can be used to assist you further with determining your grandparents' death dates. I call this type of research Sibling Searches.

Sibling Searches

When you reach a dead-end in your research, this type of search can be very helpful. A particular advantage to this type of researching is that it is not restricted to any specific time period. The only requirement is that the ancestor you are researching must have had brothers or sisters. Fortunately for us, it has only been since the last 30 to 40 years that people have not had fairly large families.

What I mean by a sibling search can be best described by giving a definition.

Sibling Search: conducting genealogy research on brothers and/or sisters of a direct ancestor.

There are several things which can be learned by conducting this type of search. If you can locate an obituary for a sibling of your ancestor it might tell you something about that person's living relatives. There may be mention of your direct ancestor, your grandparent in this case, about where he is currently living. Here the sibling search refers to your grandparents' brothers and sisters (your great-aunts and great-uncles).

The death certificate of a sibling may list who the parents were and the date and place of the sibling's birth. The parents are your ancestor's parents as well and the sibling's birth place may also be your ancestor's birth place. If your ancestor's birth place is somewhere else you still have learned where the family was living the year of the sibling's birth.

Example #3

Let's say that you are researching your grandfather and have reached a dead-end. You know that he was a middle child of six, but your information about his birth is sketchy. You know his death date but the town where he died didn't issue death certificates until 7 years later. You're stuck right! Maybe not if you try a sibling search. Research the younger children just as you would your grandfather. If you can determine one of their death dates and places, you may be able to obtain their death certificate or obituary. This could be true if the brother or sister was living in a different town than your grandfather when they died. The time when death certificates were first kept on record for this town or any other is probably different than for the town where your grandfather died. Having the sibling's death certificate may inform you as to where they were born. This location could quite possibly be the same place where your grandfather was born!

If one or more of the brothers and sisters lived longer than your grandfather it might increase the chances that a death certificate exist for them. In fact, every resource mentioned for locating information about your direct ancestor should be checked here as well. It not only makes your files more complete but it really does work!

Grandparents Marriage Information

When you start searching for your grandparents' marriage record you should first ask yourself the question "how and where did grandpa meet grandma?" The places you should check and the procedures you should follow are:

1) The city where your grandmother was born. Most marriages occured in the city where the bride was living just prior to the wedding. If this is the same city where she was born then you have it.

2) The city where the oldest child of your grandparents was born. Quite often the first child was born within a year or two of the parents' wedding. People didn't move around as much 50 or more years ago which is to the researchers advantage. Achieving success here could require conducting a sibling search.

Reverse Genealogy Research

For a majority of your research, this time period may be of minimal interest to you unless you are conducting what I call "reverse genealogy research." By this I mean researching forwards in time from a distant ancestor to the present via one or more of his descendant lines. This is the opposite of "conventional genealogy research" in which your research starts with you and you work backwards in time to your ancestors.

There are two reasons why you would conduct this type of research: 1) to locate who your distant cousins are, third, fourth, and fifth for example, and 2) to determine some or all of the descendants of a particular ancestor or ancestor pair. Both of these will take a considerable amount of time, especially the second case if the ancestor you start from was born in the 1600s.

You will find that researching reverse genealogy after 1910 is much more difficult than you would expect. The reason being that you do not always have access to the records you need to locate the people you are looking for. Think of the difficulty that the police forces of today have locating someone who just disappears from a town and you will get the general idea of what I am talking about.

Locating Distant Cousins

If you are interested in learning who your distant cousins are, you should proceed as follows. I will use an example here which describes the research path you should follow.

Globally what you are doing is making a "U-turn" in your research. You start with yourself, and work back to your parents, grandparents, great-grandparents and so forth. Now go sideways by selecting a brother or sister of one of your ancestors. This person would be a great-great- . . . aunt or uncle to you. From this person you determine who all of their descendants are until you get back to your generation. Whoever these people are who share the same generation as yourself, will be your distant cousins.

Example #4

Let me use your great-grandmother, on your mother's mother's side, as the example. By going sideways you select one of her brother's, Jerry. You learn that Jerry married and had five children, one of them being Charlie. By the way, Charlie and his brothers and sisters are your grandmother's first cousins. Charlie married and had three children; Daniel, Marjorie and Elizabeth. These three people are your mother's second cousins. Of them, Marjorie married and had four children; William, Christine, Susan and Timothy. You probably have figured it out already that these four people are your third cousins. When you reach this point the U-turn is complete.

You may find some surprising things when you determine who your distant cousins are. For example, these third cousins described above could be 40 years older or younger than you are. When I conducted a search like this, I learned that my grandmother on my mother's side has a first cousin who is 54 years younger than she is! What a surprise that was.

The interesting part of all this, in my opinion, is that these people are around today, living as doctor's or city planners or even the restaurant owner around the corner.

Complete Descendants Searches

The other reason for conducting a reverse genealogy search is to create a complete descendants listing of a particular ancestor.

This may not sound like much at first but consider the following. A simple example of one of these descendants listings is if you make a list of your parents, all of their children and spouses, all of their children and spouses and all of their children (and spouses) until you run out of people. For me the list includes ten people to date and it is only for three generations! Now imagine how many people you would be locating if the person you started from lived in 1707. You can quickly appreciate the amount of work required to complete this type of search.

After you have gathered this information, you should compile it into a book and publish it. This is a fairly common form of creating a genealogy resource on your family name. This will allow other genealogists to benefit from your hard work. By the way, another name for these complete descendants searches is a compiled genealogy which is discussed in a later chapter.

Published family/surname genealogies are one of the most valuable resources of any I have described to the genealogist. I probably cannot express just how important these resources are in words here. You will have to experience for yourself the feeling you get when you first connect one of your ancestors to one of those published in a compiled family genealogy. Making this one connection could lead you to the discovery of dozens of direct ancestors. Even though making such a connection occurs rarely I have been successful four or five times and it is a thrill every time.

A word of caution about using these compiled genealogies is required here. Don't assume that just because the information is published and on the shelves in the library that all the information is correct. You should check some or all of it with the other resources I have previously discussed. Although errors can and do occur, I have found that a very high percentage of all the information published in these books to be correct. Most people who went to the trouble of publishing family genealogies, were extremely careful about the accuracy of every fact in it.

A point worth noting if you plan on tackling this project of a complete descendants search. Locating all the descendants of a particular ancestor is a lot of hard work, and I don't mean this lightly. Unless you are the only child of an only child of an only child of an only child of an only child, you are in for a lengthy project. Most probably your ancestors had 4 to 8 children who in turn had 4 to 8 children,who in turn had 4 to 8 children, and so on. It has only been recently, the past 40 years or so, that people started having smaller families. Unfortunately this makes for a lot of work for you, the genealogist.

To give you an idea of the numbers of people possible consider the following. If you assume 28 years per generation and start with a person that was born in 1850, six generations later, which will take you to the 1980s, you could have as many as 1600 descendants from this one person! This doesn't include any spouses, and I only assumed 4 children for every generation. The numbers are probably somewhat smaller than this because not every child has children. This is by no means a discussion to discourage this type of research. I encourage anyone who has the persistence to follow through on a project like this. Good luck!

Detailed Discussion of Resources

State Censuses

I will defer the discussion of these records until the third chapter. The reason being that there were only a few state censuses conducted after 1910. Besides, many of the other resources discussed here have a greater potential for yielding useful genealogy information for this time period (present to 1910).

Vital Records

Birth, marriage and death records are three of the most official documents that the genealogy researcher has access to. Public access to any of these records is strictly dependant upon the state in which the records are located. For example, access to these records in Connecticut is impossible unless you are a member of a Connecticut Genealogical Society. You also must search for the records yourself or hire someone who is a member and is willing to do the search for you. In Massachusetts the rules are quite a bit more flexible allowing a much broader audience with looser time restrictions than those imposed by New York State discussed earlier in this chapter.

Some of the information found on these records may be

more important than you first realize. For example, you may learn who the parents of a person are through a birth record and not notice or remember at a later time, that the record also mentions the father's occupation. At first, knowing his occupation may not seem very important but it could turn out to be the one fact that helps you to break into his genealogy. Remember that a person's occupation defines life-style, habits and family movement.

More specifically, the information that you may find on these records is given below.

birth record:
    name of child
    birth date and place
    parent's names, age and birth place
    father's occupation
    number of mother's children
    medical attendant
    color or race

marriage record:
    name of husband and wife
    couple's ages, birth dates and places
    parents' names, birth dates and places
    marriage date and place
    marriage official and witness
    current address

death record:
    deceased's name
    death date and place
    age at death
    birth date and place
    occupation
    marital status at death
    parents' names and birth places
    cause of death
    medical attendant
    place of burial

I mentioned above that you may find some of this information on the records which you locate. Every state and every city or town has a different form for each of these records.

This means, of course, that the information contained on any one of these records will depend upon where it is kept on file. Very few of them will contain all of the items I have listed. You won't know for sure what your specific record will contain until you have a copy in hand.

Newspaper Articles

The use of newspaper vital record notices in genealogy research has the potential of supplying a great deal of useful information. The condition which determines their usefulness is, of course, dependant upon the newspaper publisher. As you might expect, the content of genealogical information varies from one newspaper to another. Some, unfortunately, carry absolutely nothing, whereas others contain names, dates, and other family information.

The reason you seek out newspapers in your researching labors is to gather information that may accompany birth, marriage, and death notices. It was fairly common 50+ years ago, and still is today, to find articles in the local papers concerning a couple's new child, or marriage, or an obituary notice that recognizes a person's life after they had died. As a guideline, I would rate the frequency of locating a newspaper published obituary the highest at about 80%, a marriage notice second at 50%, and a birth notice the lowest at 10%. This may give you some assistance as to how successful you might be when you are trying to locate this type of record.

Before you can utilize this resource in your research, you MUST know the date of the article you are searching for. Without knowing the exact birth, marriage, or death date, you could be in for a lengthy search followed by a big disappointment. You, yourself, will have to decide whether or not it is worth the time and effort to search for an article if you do not know the exact date. Searching through a weeks worth of newspapers is definitely worth the effort, but maybe not a whole month's worth.

Where in the newspaper should you look for these articles? The index, which should be on the first page, is a very good place to start if one exists. If not, then you will have to read the whole paper to determine what section contains the local notices. The obituaries, birth and marriage notices should be found in this section. After you have checked through several papers, you will learn roughly where these articles and notices can be found in that particular newspaper.

I should state that searching a whole week for an article is actually very good research practice. There are no set rules which govern when a newspaper published a vital record notice, if at all. For example, if you have a death date of July 17, 1931, you should search the newspapers from the 17th to the 24th for an obituary. If it is not found after a seven day time period, then you have to decide whether or not to continue searching. Many newspapers were very sloppy when it came to reporting any type of vital record notice.

You should be aware of both the obvious differences between newspapers from different cities and towns, as well as the subtle changes within a particular newspaper itself that occurred over the course of many years. Do not assume that since the newspaper published obituaries in the 1960s that they also published them in the 1920s. The personnel changes that occurred over the course of forty years could have had a major impact on whether or not these notices were published. The librarian or local historian may know something about the informational content of the local newspapers.

Trick #2

When you are searching for vital record notices, you must be aware of the possibility of a separate article written specifically about the person. These primarily accompany death notices, however, it is possible to locate an article about a marriage announcement on occasion. The following discussion will be referring to an article that may accompany an obituary. It applies equally to articles found with birth and marriage notices.

There are two conditions which would increase the chances of the existence of such an article. The first concerns the population of the city or town where the person died at the time of their death. If it was a "small town" (population less than 5,000), then "everybody knew everybody else," as they say, and a death is big news. When this did happen, the local newspaper often printed a nice article about the person and their life.

The second condition concerns the community prominence

of the person. The more socially prominent a person is, whether it be politically, religiously, or personally such as living to a great age, the more likely the local newspaper printed an article about them. The existence of such an article is something that you may not even be aware of until you locate one!

These articles could mention some family history, local social and occupational information, personal life-style, and living relatives. The whole trick here is to remember that these articles may exist and to look for them.

Telephone and City/Town Directories

You may wish to consider checking city/town directories as one of your first resources when you are researching a family for the first time in a new city or town. The reason for this is as follows. When you are trying to find the location where a person was born, you should ask yourself the question "how do I go about searching and where do I start looking for information?"

The ideal resource for this would be a complete index of names of all the people, including children, living in the town for a particular year. This, of course, never exists for any town, but city directories come close to filling this need if they exist. Typically these directories list the head of household, current home address and sometimes a business address. The advantage to using directories is that you can check very quickly whether or not the family or person you are researching was residing in that town for a given year. Since most of these are listed alphabetically, you can locate a person as quickly as you can look up someone's telephone number in your latest telephone book.

The biggest drawback to most of these directories, is that they are probably only located at the main library within that particular city or town. If the town is very small, then the largest library in that county will carry the directories for that town if they exist at all. Even so, this means that you will either have to visit the library yourself or have someone do the research for you.

Sometimes a second source for locating your city directories is the county historical society. If you contact a larger library in the county and ask them at their reference department how to contact the historical society for that county, they should be able to supply you with an address or telephone number or both. The availability of these directories is strictly dependant upon the state and county you are researching in.

When you are searching through city/town directories, always record the address your person is residing at for the following reasons. It was very common in the 1930s and years previous, to have several adults and possibly their families living at the same address. If this did occur, more than likely those people listed are all related one way or another. By noting the home address each year for your person, and looking for other people with the same surname at the same address, you may find the above to be true. If so, then you may have located additional relatives at no extra charge!

By following your person back year by year in the directories, you can determine the first year they appeared in that city or town. Similarly, by following your person forwards year by year, you can determine the last year they appeared. This will bracket them for a period of time when they were living in that city or town. The following example should clarify exactly what I mean.

Example #5

Let us say that your mother was born in 1917 in Town-1. Starting in the 1917 city directory for Town-1, look for her father, your grandfather, in the listings. If he is listed, look for him in the 1918, 1919, . . . directories until he is no longer listed. Also look through the 1916, 1915, 1914, . . . directories until he again disappears. This will locate him in this town for a bracket of years.

If he is not listed for the year your mother was born, you should check through the other years anyway. Sometimes several related families lived together for a while until one or more of them could support themselves on their own. When this happened, the head of household would be the only person listed in the directory. Your grandfather could have been living with a brother, sister, or other relative for a short time. You must remember that just because the person isn't listed in the directory for this year, it doesn't mean that they were not living in the town.

Another thing you may find, is some of the earlier directories gave a death date for a person who was listed in the directory for the previous year. This is ideal if it happens for you because that is exactly what you are looking for. It is very possible that if your grandfather died in 1911, the 1911 directory probably has a listing for him. The 1912 directory may have him listed, but only for the reason of listing his death date. The 1913, 1914, . . . directories will not have him listed in any capacity. If your grandmother was still living in 1913 she would be listed in that year's directory.

Trick #3: City Directory Surname Listings

An important comment about the use of these directories is needed here. You should always write down or photocopy every person that has your mother's father's (for this example) surname. Listed along with your grandfather could very well be his father or mother, an uncle, or brothers and sisters. Writing down everybody with the same surname the first time will prevent having to go back at a later date to the same directory when you are looking for your great-grandfather. Granted you may not know which of these people listed, if any, are related to your grandfather, but that will become clear with a little more work.

Let me cite another example here which will help you in determining the death date.

Example #6: Determining The Death Date

You have learned that Mr. G is listed in the city directories for 1913 and before but not in 1914 or after. You suspect that since he was at least 65 years old in 1913 that he may have died that year and that is the reason why he is not listed in the 1914 directory. To proceed from here, you should make use of one or more of the following: a death record, newspaper obituary, church records, or cemetery records. You don't want to have to search through all these records if you don't have to, so which one should you start with. As I have mentioned, that unless you know the exact date of death it may not be advantageous to try for a death record or an obituary.

For this situation you are looking for a complete list of names of people who died in 1913. As mentioned, such an index probably doesn't exist but cemetery records come about as close as you are going to get besides city directories. This leads us into the next resource, cemetery records.

Cemetery Records

The records at any cemetery contain a list of people who are interred on their grounds. With a full name and approximate year of death, the cemetery patron can tell you whether or not that person is buried there. Once you locate the correct cemetery, you will know at least the burial date. The death date was then a day or two before the burial date. Now you should go back to the other resources mentioned and search for those records. This task should be much easier now that you know the exact date of death.

Cemetery records are probably the best resource, of those available, for determining the exact death date when you are not sure just what it is. The reasons for this are twofold. First, for this time period, death certificates may not be public access records. As I mentioned in the vital records discussion, availability of death certificates is decided by the laws of the state in which they were filed. If the state you are researching in does allow public access to death certificates, then obtaining this document should be pursued as the first step once you know the exact date of death. If you do not have access to a death certificate then you will have to use another resource.

The second reason for searching through cemetery records, is their global nature. By this I mean, one cemetery could have hundreds of thousands of people buried in it spanning a hundred years or more. Loosely speaking, each cemetery contains a separate index of names of people.

You must be aware of the fact that not all the people found in a particular cemetery died in the town where the cemetery is located. Many families have a "family plot" in a cemetery, and you may find them all buried there whether or not they all died there. This is an important point worth noting because it may save you wasted research time.

Sometimes when you are searching for a death date, you may not even know the year of death. Obviously this makes the researching more difficult. If you can bracket a section of 5 to 10 years that the person died within, the clerk at the cemetery office can probably locate the record. You should always try to get as close as possible to the correct year of death BEFORE you contact the cemetery office requesting a search. This will minimize the amount of searching the clerk has to do for you.

The reason the clerk prefers the exact year of death, is that most of the cemeteries I have dealt with have their records arranged by year and not alphabetically by surname. This is true especially for the larger cemeteries which have 100,000 or more people interred in them. This may be beginning to change with computers becoming so popular and inexpensive. If a cemetery does have their records stored on a computer file, then they would have access to any person very quickly just by entering their name. But until computers are more widely used in this capacity, you must remember that their records are probably arranged by year.

Statement of Importance

You should always make it as easy as possible for the clerk who has to search for the record you want. They are more than likely conducting searches for many other people who are researching their own family history. All of this is in addition to their regular work!

Locating The Correct Cemetery

Once you have decided that cemetery records are the most appropriate resource to search through next, you need to locate the one in which your ancestor is buried. Knowing the person's religion will probably narrow the field down to less than a handful. You should start by calling the cemetery offices (if one exists) of the cemeteries located in the city/town where your person was last listed in the city directory. Even if you are not sure of their religion the number of telephone calls you will have to make should be small.

If you do not locate the correct cemetery right away you should try those located in neighboring towns. For some of the smaller cemeteries that do not have an on sight office, you may have to contact the municipal clerks office to learn where and who is keeping the records. Remember to include alternate spellings of your ancestor's surname when you ask someone to conduct a search. Some cemeteries have no formal records at all which means that you will have to make a trip to the cemetery grounds and conduct the search on foot by reading headstone inscriptions.

If you are still unable to locate the correct cemetery then one of three things may have occurred: 1) there is no record of your ancestor's burial even though they may have died there, 2) they are buried in a town in which you have not yet searched, 3) the year your ancestor died was outside of the range of years you searched. At this point it may make more sense to use another resource to try to learn more information about when and where your ancestor died.

I must add a personal note here about using cemetery records as a research tool. Over the past few years, I have searched through dozens of cemeteries looking for ancestors, and I have found this part of the research to be one of the most interesting. The variety of locations, terrain, age of the cemeteries, types of headstones and inscriptions is almost limitless. This is a part of history that many people never see or experience. I highly recommend visiting the cemeteries where your ancestors are buried as well as any of the larger or older ones within your visiting distance.

Church Records

The three obvious types of information you might find in church records are baptisms, marriages and burials. On occasion you may find an ancestor who was an active member of the church, such as deacon, chorus, etc. More often than not, however, you will be using church records for determining the dates and names that accompany the central person on baptism and marriage records.

For this time period you should have no trouble locating records if you know one thing. That is, of course, the name of the church. This may sound like a small detail but consider that a city of 100,000 people may have 50 or more churches of all denominations. The county in which I currently live, Monroe County, New York, had a population of just over 700,000 people in 1980. The total number of churches within this county numbered at least 393! (I counted all those I found in the telephone book). The last thing you want to do is check with every one of these churches for information that has a chance of not even existing.

The task at hand is to reduce the total number of churches to a more reasonable level of ten or less. The most obvious way is by the person's denomination; Jewish, Catholic, Presbyterian, Methodist, and so forth. Merely knowing this may reduce the number of possible choices to a handful. If this is the case, then you should contact each church one-by-one requesting the information you are looking for. However, if knowing the denomination only reduces the number to a dozen or more, then you could try one of three things

First, try to learn the exact church name from another source. Obituary notices and cemetery records are ideal for this. The obituaries usually mention where services will be held and what funeral home will be handling the arrangements. If the former is true then you have the name of the church. If the funeral home is mentioned, then you should contact them and ask if they have in their records the name of the church which conducted the services.

Second, try to locate the person or people in the city directory for the year of interest. This means the year the person was baptized, married, or died. Why will looking in city directories help you here? You may be able to learn the person's home address! The reason this is important is that most people, even today, do not travel all the way across town to attend church. This was especially true 50+ years ago when the mode of transportation was something other than the family station wagon. Today people tend to stick with a particular church parish if the drive isn't too terribly long. So, if you were to look for a church that was fairly close to your person's home, Catholic by parish for example, you may locate the one which they attended.

Third, try to eliminate all those churches that were founded after the date you are interested in. In other words, any church whose records do not go back far enough in history to your date, could not be the one you are looking for. The drawback with this suggestion is, you will have to contact each church in order to learn the year in which they were founded. This really isn't all that tedious because you can simply ask the clerk what year their records start. If the dates don't match, then you have your answer, NO!

From one of these three suggestions, you should be able to narrow the field of choices to a very manageable number.

A couple of words of caution about church records is needed here. Some of the older churches may have lost part of their records in fires. The church may be 150 years old but their records only go back to 1919 because of a fire that occurred in 1918. It is unfortunate that this information is lost forever but this type of situation exists when dealing with very old records. Still other churches have closed which means that their records may have been transferred to local denominational archives.

The other thing to be careful of, is the work load of the church office clerks. Naturally, they will be busy with their routine church matters and may not have the time to search for your information. I have found that most church office clerks will do a search for you when they are not so busy. It may take several days or a week or two, but they usually can find time for your request. I personally wish to thank all of these people who have assisted me with my research.

Family Bibles

Family Bibles can range in usefulness as a research tool from being absolutely no help whatsoever to containing a wealth of valuable information. This range in usefulness is really not surprising if you remember that all types of people from all over the country (world) could possibly have kept vital family information in their Bible. It strictly depends upon the interest of the person(s) who owned the Bible.

The type of information that you typically find is names of family members, their baptism or birth date, marriage date or death date. This information may be written on the inside cover or sometimes you find separate pieces of paper tucked inside the pages. With these separate pages you may also find official baptism certificates or maybe even a marriage certificate. If the person was very tedious about their information gathering they may have included some photographs.

Another problem with Bibles as a resource other than informational content is their availability. Many people did not keep Bibles at all. Others who did have had their's lost through the years of moving and handing down personal belongings from one generation to another.

In spite of these problems, they should be sought after for every family household you research. You should ask your parents, grandparents and aunts and uncles if they remember anyone who kept such a Bible.

Land and Mortgage Records

These records can usually be found at the town/county clerk's office in the town/county where the property is located. If you are unable to reach this office, the clerk at the reference desk at the county library should be able to assist you with locating where these records are kept on file.

Why might you consider checking these records in your genealogy research? I can think of two reasons. First, since these are legal documents, they tend to be written rather formally much like a will. This formality, often times, gives the full names of both the seller and the buyer. If a husband and wife buy a house or property together, more than likely both their full names will appear on the document.

The second reason concerns the date of the transaction. Knowing the exact date when a person bought or sold property can help to determine the number of years the person(s) resided at a particular location. This may not seem important, but it could help you. There will be times in your research when the person you are researching just disappears as previously mentioned. You may have "tabs" on him for 10 or 20 years and then he is just gone. Land and mortgage records might be able to help you narrow the time span which you have him located.

As I mentioned earlier, it was very common before the 1930s for the father and/or mother to move in with one of their children after they retired. Naturally when this occurs, they would sell any of their property or at least transfer the titles to one or more of the children. In any case, they probably will not appear in any city records after they move in.

If the person died then you would think that a death certificate or cemetery record would exist. If this were the case, then any property would change ownership through the execution of the will.

The most difficult situation to research occurs when the family moved out of town. To find out where they moved to, and this could be just about anywhere, you need to find mention of it in a record somewhere. The last property record will tell you the date when the family was last living in that town. This can assist you when you try to locate where they have moved to. You will know NOT to search for the family anywhere else before this last date. This can only help to pinpoint the years which you need to conduct further research. Sometimes these records will give the current or forwarded address. If this happens then you have exactly what you are looking for, their new location!

Wills

Wills are an extremely important resource for confirming the relationships of family members. Sometimes it is the only source available which confirms who the parents are of a particular individual.

Wills are typically located at the surrogate court house in the town, the county seat of the county, where the death took place. If the town is fairly small, this office may be the same as the municipal clerk's office. You can learn where the wills are on file by writing or calling the municipal clerk's office in the town where the person died and asking the clerk where they are located.

The biggest plus for using wills as a research tool, is their potential for listing children's names, brothers and sisters, in-laws, and other relatives and friends who were recipients of items listed in its contents. From this one document, you may learn the relationships of several people you are researching.

However, there are a couple of problems with using wills as a resource. First, is their existence at all for any individual. Not everyone made out a will 50+ years ago. Today it is much more common which is great for those who will be researching their family history 50 years from now. This won't help you now, of course, and the best I can do for you here, is to say that you will just have to check to see if one exists for your person.

The second problem concerns their informational content. Sometimes everything is left to the spouse with absolutely no mention at all about children. It could be as simple as a single sentence where the person makes a global statement leaving everything to one named person. It is almost chance that decides whether or not a will exists at all and how informative its contents will be.

MR. G

TOPICS:

basic research procedures

discussion of the period's two parts

helpful research tricks

spelling of surnames

the logic of the research

AVAILABLE RESOURCES:

birth/marriage/death records   IGI

cemetery records   • immigration indices

church records   land/mortgage records

city/town directories   • military records

compiled early settlers indices   newspapers

compiled genealogies   ship passenger lists

• compiled town histories   • soundex

family Bibles   telephone directories

• federal & state censuses   wills

• denotes the resources discussed in this chapter

1910 TO 1790

Research Procedures

When you get to this time period in your research (1910–1790), you will probably be two or more generations back. It really doesn't make any difference which generation you are researching because the techniques apply equally to all. As I mentioned previously, the information you are interested in, no matter what generation you are researching, is dates and places of births, marriages and deaths, spouses and children. The only difference in researching between time periods is the resources available to the researcher.

You may ask yourself where to start when your research enters this time period? You should always, no matter what time period you are researching, start your search in the town where you last have record of your person. From here you should decide which resources you want to search through first. The items you should consider for this are:

1) date/year you are researching in,

2) population of city/town, and

3) state you are researching in.

All of these will effect the availability of a given resource. Once you are familiar with their availability for a particular year, state and town, you should be able to increase your research efficiency. By this I mean, make the most effective use of your time. You will still have to use your best judgement for every ancestor to decide which resources are the most beneficial to search through first. In general I suggest the following two steps.

Step #1

Of the resources listed at the beginning of this chapter, I

suggest starting with vital records (births, marriages, deaths) if
they are available. One must, however, know the town and year
where the record is filed. These records can immediately inform
you of pertinent dates and places. Refer to the detailed discussion
on vital records in the second chapter.

Step #2

If you do not know the town, or the records don't exist, try
checking censuses, both federal and state, city/town directories,
and cemetery records. As I discuss later, I believe that census
records are one of the most useful resources for this time period.
They have the potential of listing the entire family by name (1850
and after).

One of the first questions you might ask concerning this
chapter is why I have chosen these particular years for the next
time period. The reason is obvious if you consider the federal
censuses as one of the primary research tools. The very first
federal census was conducted in 1790 for eleven states and the
1910 census is the most recent census available to the general
public to date for all 50 states (the 1920 federal census will be
available in 1992). It is interesting to note that even though Alaska
and Hawaii were not officially declared states until almost sixty
years later there are censuses for each of them in 1910. Federal
censuses can be so useful that I have tailored this time period to
their starting and ending dates.

The resources which are available to you for this time period
include some of those described in the previous chapter. The
discussion of compiled genealogies is put off until the next
chapter for reasons which are discussed in that chapter. How you
make use of any of these resources and what information they
may contain is basically the same. Specific points about any of
them which are unique to this time period will be discussed.

One point needs to be mentioned up front about these
resources, which really concerns genealogy research in general.
You will find that as you push a family name further back in time,
the usefulness of a particular resource diminishes. If you consider
the years when each state was admitted to the Union you soon
realize that some records will be dated after their admittance.
There were people living in each state before these dates but there

may not be any records on these people. To explain what I mean by this let me cite another example.

Example #7

Assume that when you were researching your grandfather, you were able to utilize city directories for the town he grew up in. From this resource you determined who his mother and father are. You now need to determine birth dates and places for each of them. You attempt to accomplish this by using city directories again, but learn that they were first printed twenty years AFTER these people were born. Obviously you can not use this resource here. This is when you will need to make use of federal and state censuses, land and mortgage records, wills, cemetery records, etc. to learn the information you are seeking. This lack of availability of the city directories eventually happens to every resource, independent of the time period you are researching in. When this happens, your only alternative is to try another resource.

The Periods Two Parts: 1910 to 1850 and 1850 to 1790

There might be a tendency to split this time period into two parts with the 1850 Federal Census being the dividing point. The reason for this is the censuses from 1850 to 1910 list by name all the family members of a particular household. This is such an extremely valuable tool to genealogy research for this time period that it is almost reason enough to separate these six censuses into a separate chapter. However, since this time period spans the full range of available federal censuses they are all grouped together for consistency.

Another comment about the early part of this time period involves the people themselves. Once you locate an ancestor or two before 1850, you may notice a residence shift eastward as your research progresses back in time. By this I mean every half century or so you research further back in time, the number of towns and states people live in diminishes and their location moves towards the 13 original colonies. The total number of people alive also diminishes as you go back in history, but this really doesn't help you all that much because there were so many people, even back then. After all, in 1700 the colonial population was 250,000 people strong, and in 1900 there were more than 76,000,000.

The point of this discussion is that your family history will tend to follow American history as long as your ancestors lived in the states. When you think about it, it really has to follow in this manner.

Spelling of Surnames

When you are using these directories, you must keep one thing in the back of your mind at all times; spelling of surnames. It happens more often than I would like that the name is misspelled or was changed by a letter or two. If at first you do not locate your person in the index, try searching under an alternate spelling. It happened quite frequently where, for a variety of reasons, a son changed the spelling of his last name by one or more letters. If this did happen, when you look up his name in any index, you have to know exactly how it was spelled or you may not find it. The more creative you are here the more successful you will be, because the number of possible misspellings can be quite high.

The spelling of surnames issue applies to every resource available to the researcher. It will catch you off guard the first time you try locating the parents (father) of one of your ancestors. You assume that what you have to go on is that the surname of your ancestor is spelled exactly the same as that of his father and mother. You know now that this is not necessarily so in the records.

Detailed Discussion of Resources

As I mentioned, most of the resources listed in this chapter were discussed in detail in the second chapter. The research methods that were outlined for the present to 1910 time period also apply here (1910 to 1790) as well. The major difference is that some of the resources will no longer be on file once you research back to their starting date. For many states this occurs in this time period for a great many of the previously mentioned resources.

Federal Censuses

The United States first conducted a census in 1790 for eleven states. Every ten years thereafter, a new census was conducted and the effort still continues today. The only census that is missing is the 1890 which was lost in a fire that occurred in January 1921 in the Commerce Department Building in Washington D.C. We genealogists have to get by with the 1880 and 1900 censuses to locate ancestors for those years. You may also have to make use of some of the other resources, such as state censuses. Although a federal census was conducted as recently as 1990, the government mandates that 72 years must pass before a federal census is released for research by the general public. They believe that this is enough time to insure public privacy to all individuals.

The type of information that you find on the more recent censuses is vastly different from the very early ones. In fact, the very first census really doesn't contain all that much information. The head of household is listed by name along with the total number of other males and all females. What you do learn from this is the state and town where the person was living in 1790. You might possibly learn a little more if you use this resource wisely. I believe this is so important that it should be followed for every available census. Trick #4 illustrates exactly what I mean.

Trick #4

After you locate your ancestor in a particular town for a given census you should search through all the people in that town for others with the same surname and record their information. The reason for this is that some or all of these families may be related to your ancestor. Recording everybody the first time you do a search will prevent having to go back to the same census at a later date.

The best way to find a library which has in its files the census for the town you are looking for is to follow the same procedure outlined in Trick #1. Merely substitute the library for the municipal clerk's office as the place you are trying to contact.

Once you have determined the correct telephone number, you should call the library during normal business hours, nine to five in most cases. With this in mind, let me mention another trick here.

Trick #5

Most of the larger libraries have a recording that answers telephone calls that come in when the library is closed. If you are calling from the east coast trying to reach the west coast, and you try calling in the morning and forget about the time zone difference, you could get their recorded message. "Why is this so bad?" It really isn't except for the telephone charges of a call made during a weekday hour. These calls, if you are not aware of it, are the most expensive of any that you can make. Why not call the library after 11pm on any night? You won't be disturbing anybody and the charges are the cheapest possible! If you do get a recording, you can probably learn what hours the library is open and plan your call accordingly. This may sound petty and hardly worth the effort, but if your ancestors are spread out all over the country, your telephone bills could add up very quickly.

When you finally do reach someone at the library, you should ask the following 4 questions:

1. Does the library have microfilm copies of the federal censuses for your county and town?
   If the answer is "NO" then you should ask what library or institution does have the records.
   If the answer is "YES" then proceed to ask question 2.

2. Do you, the researcher, have access to the censuses?
   If the answer is "NO," ask follow up questions on who does have access and how you can obtain information contained in the census.
   If the answer is "YES" then proceed to the next question.

3. Can someone at the library get the information for you? In other words, will they search through the microfilm for your people.
   If the answer is "NO" then proceed to question 4.
   If the answer is "YES" then ask what the fees are and how long it will take someone to get the information.

4. Does the library have a list of people who do genealogy research for a fee?

If the answer is "NO" then you are stuck!

If the answer is "YES" then ask if they would send a copy of the list to you.

When you are finished with the above questions you should know the following:

1) if the records exist at all,

2) where the records are located, and

3) how to obtain information contained on them.

You now have to go ahead and follow up on getting this information if you decide it is worth the time and effort.

Step #1: Determining the Correct Roll of Microfilm

For each of the censuses from 1790 to 1860, an index of all head-of-household names that appear in the census exists for every state that conducted a census. Before you get to the microfilm reader with the roll of film you have selected to search through, you should try to locate your person in these indices. The index will tell you on what page your person can be found. If you are going to be searching through a census that does not have an index, 1870 or later, proceed to step #2. Otherwise proceed to step #3 and load your roll of microfilm onto the reader.

Step #2: Determining the Town

Now it is time to search through the microfilm to try to locate your person. But before you load the film onto the reader I strongly suggest that you try to determine the town your ancestor lived in. Knowing the town can greatly reduce the amount of searching you may have to do. If you were unable to learn the town but you know the county then you can proceed to the reader but be prepared for what may be a lengthy search.

The reason you may have to search through the entire county or town for your person is that not one of the rolls of microfilm for any census, federal or state, lists the people alphabetically. The people are arranged by town, and ward for the larger cities, but they are listed randomly within each town or ward.

Searching through an entire town really isn't all that bad as long as the town's population is less than a few thousand people.

If the town or city is fairly large, it is probably separated into numbered wards. You can determine which ward you should search through by knowing the street address your person lived on that year. The large cities have ward maps which show what ward a particular street was located in.

To determine the street your person lived on the year of the census, refer to the city directories for that year. Merely look up your person in the directory, just as you would look up someone today in the telephone book. The street address will be listed next to their name and you can proceed from there.

If you are unable to determine the street your person lived on, then you are probably stuck with looking through every ward for that city. This is when you will have to decide whether or not conducting this lengthy a search is really worth your time and effort. It may make more sense to pursue other resources and come back to the censuses at a later date.

I have one last suggestion which might help you here. Try to locate your person in the city directories for a couple of years either side of the year of the census. For example, if you are searching in the 1900 census, check the city directories from 1897 to 1903 for your person. He/she may be listed in a year other than 1900 for a number of reasons. If a listing still does not exist, then you are stuck searching through the entire town.

Step #3: Using the Census Records

Once you have selected the proper roll of microfilm, you need to put it on a reader and start your search. If you are unfamiliar with the use of a microfilm reader, ask one of the librarians to assist you.

After you have the reader set up, you should start your search with the following:

1) the page number your person is on, if you made use of an index,

2) page one of the town your person was living in if known, and

3) the first page of the roll of microfilm otherwise.

Scroll through the film until you locate the correct page from above. Once you reach the correct page, search down through all the names on the page until you find your persor or have to go to the next page.

Remembering that the people are not listed alphabetically in any town or city ward may help you to decide just how long to search through a particular roll of microfilm. Trick #6 may help to make the searching go a little quicker.

Trick #6

Let me add a helpful hint here about reading through hundreds and hundreds of hand written names. When you have to search through an entire town, you want to be able to search as quickly as possible. Try to focus on the last names only when you scan down the list. Once you locate the correct surname, you then read the first names to see if you have located the right family. If you try reading full names, it will take you much longer than is necessary. After a dozen pages or so, your ability to focus on only the surnames should be quite good.

As I mentioned, the 1790 census generally contains a very small amount of useful genealogical information. This is NOT to say that what it tells you is of no value. It is valuable for what it does tell you! Besides learning the town and number of other family members, you might possibly learn the names of still other family members if you again make use of Trick #4 by looking for anybody with the same surname.

The 1800 through 1840 censuses contain a little more information but they still are somewhat limited in their usefulness. They too only list the head-of-household by name but now they separate the rest of the family into 10 year age groups. As these censuses progressed, the number of age group divisions increased with the 1840 containing the most. Refer to one or more of the references listed in the bibliography for more information. I suggest *The Source* for starters, since it contains a complete discussion of these censuses.

The remaining censuses, 1850 to 1910, are the most useful and are very important resources when conducting genealogy research. Each of these censuses list ALL the family members of a particular household by name. This is extremely useful because if you locate an ancestor as a child in a census, you will more than likely find them listed along with their parents and brothers and sisters. It is very possible through a single census to locate the next generation of a particular family line.

The phrase "family member" should be clarified here. When you locate your ancestral family in a census, you must not assume that all the people listed living in that household are directly related to one another. It was fairly common in the 1800s for cousins, in-laws, sometimes a very close friend or even a maid, to be listed with a family other than their own. Some of the censuses give the relationship of everybody listed, to the head-of-household. This will make determining relationships a much easier task. For those censuses that do not give relationships, you will have to use other resources to determine exactly how the people listed are related.

Other information which you may find in these censuses are an individual's age, state/county or country where they were born, occupation and state where their mother and father were born. It is true that the 1910 census offers a little more information than does the 1850, but the greatest asset to all of these censuses from 1850 to date is that they list everyone by name.

Immigration Indices

Immigration indices are basically lists of people who immigrated to the US from their homeland for a particular span of years. This resource is, for all intents and purposes, the last resource which you would use for a particular ancestor. The reason is, as stated earlier, that once you locate the immigrant ancestor for a particular family line, your work is finished. The unfortunate thing about these resources is they are not as common as I would like for this time period. I believe the vast numbers of people that came to America in the 1800s is what has limited their existence. For example, between 1800 and 1929 there were more than 35,000,000 immigrants to America, 9,000,000 of whom arrived between 1880 and 1900 (Britannica 946, 274). To have all these people catalogued and published would be a monumental task. Some of the indices that do exist are listed in the bibliography.

When you start to use these resources you should already have a rough idea of the date and country from which your ancestor immigrated. This could have been learned from federal

Example #8

or state censuses under the place born, father born or mother born columns.

If your person was born in Pennsylvania circa 1840 and the 1880 census lists him and his family naming Ireland as the birth place of both his parents, you know that his parents came to America sometime before 1840. If you assume 28 years per generation, then his parents were born around 1812 which means that they probably immigrated after 1830. This gives you a span of ten years in which they more than likely came to America. To allow for possible errors in the recorded dates, you should expand the search by five or ten years on either side. I suggest starting your search with your best guess year and working from there.

Trick #7

The previous example is not completely accurate for the following reason. It is entirely possible that the people who were born in Ireland circa 1812 came to America a year or two after they were born with their own parents! The only information the 1880 census gave you was the place of birth. You must not assume that since they were foreign born that they immigrated when they were adults. It is very possible that they and each of their parents immigrated when they were children. Always try to keep this in mind when using these records.

Another possibility is that your person may not be listed at all in any of these indices. The success of finding your person is somewhat dependant upon the year of immigration and country from which they came. Some years have a substantial number of catalogued immigrants from a wide range of countries. Other years have almost nothing. You will have to determine what the appropriate years are to learn what indices are available.

Compiled Town Histories

These resources can range in usefulness from "a total waste of time" to "as valuable as the air you are breathing" (not really but almost). This strictly depends upon the author who compiled the information about the early people of the town. A majority of these books were written 50 to 150 years ago by a wide variety of "qualified" people; town historians, professional genealogists, commissioned printers.

The content and organization also varies greatly. Some of the writers not only included facts about the first settlements of the area, but also biographical facts about the first people who participated in the town's settlement. For genealogy purposes, these biographical sections are of the most interest. They usually inform you when the different municipal buildings were erected, when the first settlers arrived and what their occupation was.

Sometimes these biographies only included information about the very first settlers and a few prominent people or families. School teachers, a clergyman, the first mayor, farmer or storekeeper, are just a few of the townspeople that may have been discussed. If your ancestor was one of these people, more than likely you will find his biography in the appropriate town history.

If, however, your ancestor(s) was just an average "Joe ancestor" like most of us, including the author, your chances of locating his biography in a compiled town history are not that high. They still should be checked out because you may just get lucky and find a lot of useful information.

The last "problem" with this resource, if I haven't mentioned enough already, is that for some towns and counties they do not exist at all. No one has yet taken the time to compile what information exists. I believe the primary reason for this is the amount of time required to gather this type of information. As I have already mentioned in a previous chapter, conducting genealogical research is very time consuming. Most of us are conducting research only on our own families. We tend to ignore the tens or possibly hundreds of other early residents who would have to be researched for the records to be complete. We should all appreciate the effort that goes into compiling one of these comprehensive town histories.

My final comments on this subject concern the good news about this resource. Every day there are more and more people getting involved with genealogy and local history. Some of the more ambitious researchers are filling in the gaps where town histories and biographies do not already exist. Even though this is a very slow process, it is happening and it will only help the "big research picture."

Military Service Records

This resource can be very helpful if you are searching for a male ancestor who was in the military at some point in his life. Obviously these records will be of little use for female ancestors and non-military people. Remember that we are dealing with times when equal rights was merely a thought in a fiction writer's mind.

There are compiled records for some of the early wars but these are usually organized by state. For example, some of the participants of the Revolutionary War are listed by the town and side they fought for. They may also be listed by their regiment or commanding officer. If your ancestor is listed, you probably will be able to learn when and who he fought for and for how long. If he died in the war, you will probably learn the date and place of death as well. The only other information pertinent to genealogical research that may be included is what state and town the soldier was from. This is, of course, extremely useful if you did not know this previously.

In general, though, there really is not an abundant amount of useful genealogical information contained in these records. The biggest reason for searching through these records, may be just to learn which ancestors fought in what wars. Wouldn't it be interesting to find out that you have an ancestor who fought with General Lee in the Civil War or fought against the British in The War of 1812? There are a number of patriotic societies whose members are descendants of war ancestors. The Daughters of the American Revolution (DAR) has a membership consisting of only those people who are descendants of ancestors who either fought in the Revolutionary War or were wartime civil servants. In genealogy circles, this is a fairly exclusive society. My daughters will automatically be eligible for membership in the DAR society since my ancestor John Chase fought in this war. A listing of some of the current genealogy societies can be found in the *Directory: Historical Agencies in North America* or the *Official Museums Directory*.

One final reason exists for researching military records, and that is to obtain a copy of your ancestor's pension records. You should refer to the publication *Military Service Records in the National Archives of the United States* for information on how to obtain these records. There may be a slight fee for this record if it exists. It would be hard for me to tell you exactly what information you can learn from a pension record because of the tremendous variation that exists from one record to another. It should at least include length of service and where he was "stationed." You will just have to check each individual record to see what additional information it contains.

To locate where any of these records are kept on file I suggest that you contact your nearest public library having a genealogy department. If they do not have the records you are looking for on their shelves, they should be able to give you an address to write to. The publication *Guide to Genealogical Research in the National Archives* contains a wealth of information on all federally sponsored resources.

State Censuses

Besides the federal censuses many states conducted their own censuses in "odd" years (years other than the 10s). *The Source* gives a very complete listing of what years each state conducted a census. You will find these recorded on microfilm along with the federal censuses in most of the larger libraries. However, most libraries only carry the census in the state and usually only the county in which the library is located. If your research takes you to a different state or county you may have to contact a library in that state or county for their state censuses. The procedure for locating and making use of these records is identical to that discussed for federal censuses.

For this time period (1910 to 1790), these records may contain some or all of the following information: spouse's name, children's name, current ages, birth dates and places, number of years married, occupation, value of house and property, and citizenship.

The 1865 NY state census contains the number of years married which is not given in the federal censuses for 1860 or 1870. Another benefit of these other year censuses, is that you may be able to decrease the number of years you have a person located. For example, if you have located a person in "Town A" in the 1860 federal census and he is not listed in the 1870 federal census, you might be able to narrow the time span of ten years to five years if you can locate him (or not) in the 1865 census (for NY State). Remember that you do learn something if your person is not listed in this census, you learn where he isn't!

The International Genealogical Index (IGI)

The International Genealogical Index (IGI) has the potential of being an extremely valuable resource when you are researching any of your ancestors who lived between the years 1500 and 1875. It is basically an index of peoples' names from more than 90 countries around the world found in the computer files of The Church of Jesus Christ of Latter-day Saints (LDS Church). The Genealogical Department of the LDS Church has been gathering information for decades and to date the index contains several million names.

The names are recorded on microfiche where they are indexed by the place of the event; birth, marriage or death. You should check with the local history and genealogy department at the closest public library to learn how to gain access to this information. If you require a more complete discussion of the IGI, refer to the publication The International Genealogical Index (IGI) published by The Family History Library.

The Logic of the Research

Nearly everything that people did was carried out for very good "logical" reasons. For example, why an ancestor suddenly appears or disappears from a particular resource, or why you are unable to locate a birth or death record all probably have very good logical reasons "why." The challenge for you is to sift through all the possible choices to learn what the truth is and why the information is not as you suspected. This is why it is called genealogy research!

The "logic" aspect to your research should be applied every time you conduct any type of genealogical search. The reason I have included the discussion here is that this may be the first time you have had to make use of the logic method with any regularity.

At first this whole idea may seem obvious to you but when you look a little deeper it may not be all that clear exactly how this applies to researching your family history. If you get stuck on a family line, stop and ask yourself a very simple logical question which applies to your situation. For example, if you are having trouble locating where an female ancestor was born, ask yourself the question how did she ever meet and marry your male ancestor? They must have been living in the same town together when they were each single for a period of time! Otherwise how would they ever have met and married? This probably means that her parents were also living in that same town! This is so obvious that you may not even think about it. Try asking yourself an appropriate, simple question when your research is leading you nowhere.

Soundex

This is a reference tool which attempts to deal with the issue of misspelled surnames for some of the federal censuses. It is called the Soundex System and it was compiled by the National Archives and the Work Projects Administration (WPA) for the 1880, 1900 and 1910 population schedules.

This filing system catalogues all surnames of the same and similar sounds but of variant spellings. By following the Soundex coding guide, described in *The Source*, you can locate a person by the sound of their surname rather than the spelling. So, in addition to all the information you would normally find in these censuses, you also learn who the people are with similar sounding names. This will help you regardless of how your ancestor's surname is spelled. You now can appreciate the value of a resource that tries to account for misspellings. An additional benefit is that it functions as an index to the censuses.

The only drawback to this resource is the availability at the libraries and the number of census schedules that have been catalogued by this system. Many of the libraries that do have the federal censuses on microfilm do not have their Soundex equivalent. You should check with your local library to try to determine the closest institution owning the Soundex.

TOPICS:

dealing with the lack of complete resources

helpful research tricks

AVAILABLE RESOURCES:

birth/marriage/death records   IGI

cemetery records   immigration indices

church records   land/mortgage records

city/town directories   military records

• compiled early settlers indices   newspapers

• compiled genealogies   ship passenger lists

compiled town histories   • special & state censuses

family Bibles   wills

• denotes the resources discussed in this chapter

1790 TO 1700

This time period is what I call the "heartbreak" section of conducting genealogy research in America. I have named it this after "Heartbreak Hill" at the 20 mile point of the Boston Marathon. Once you push a family line back beyond this time period, before 1700, you are 90% finished with the work and it is a breeze from there—not really but close. In researching my own genealogy, I have found this time period to be the most difficult to obtain information in and a family line stopper on more than one occasion.

From these statements you are probably wondering why I have labeled this time period so harshly. The reason is, as you might expect, a direct result of the availability, or more accurately, the lack of the availability of resources. The length of the list of resources is deceiving in its usefulness because most of them are what I call local "global" resources. By this I mean the records are on file by town or county and sometimes by state but they only cover the larger or well populated areas. This means that you will have to know the correct location in order to find the records for your ancestor. Moreover, the resources that are listed are not as complete as they are for the previous time period (1910 to 1790).

How this effects your research can be seen more directly in the following situation. It sometimes occurs, especially in this time period, that an ancestor just seems to "show up" in a town. With most of the resources being incomplete or missing, it makes it more difficult to determine exactly where this person came from. One of my ancestors, Talmadge Edwards, just shows up in Johnstown,New York in 1770. I have yet to find a reference stating where he came from or a record of any sort from any state listing him as a child of "Whoever" Edwards. This is one of my dead ends that has frustrated me for several years. This problem is one of the biggest reasons why this time period is such a difficult one to conduct research in.

Another thing you will find is that people moved around a lot, always pushing further westward as the decades passed by. This makes the researching even more difficult.

When you get stuck like this on one person, you should do the following, especially if it is in this time period. Stop and think for a few minutes about everything you know about this person. I suggest that you make a separate brand new list on a clean sheet of paper paying particular attention to the smallest detail or piece of information.

Example #9

Using my ancestor as the example, let me illustrate what I mean. When I was unable to make any progress after several months, I asked myself the following questions: what year does he first appear in the town, how old was he that year, was he single or married, were there any brothers or sisters who showed up with him that same year, if so how old were they, what religion were they, is there a will on record for him or any of his siblings and if so can birth years be learned from them, are there cemetery records, was he a citizen of the United States, etc? An answer to any of these questions may be sufficient to lead you to new and valuable information. So far for my ancestor they have yielded little additional information but I am confident that something will eventually turn up.

Once you know some of the personal information about your ancestor you need to work out a strategy for what to do next. You want to start with resources which have alphabetical listings of as many people as possible. This way you can look up the surname, Edwards, in my case, and see who was alive and when, about the time he was born. The "when" is important here because the dates have to make sense. If you suspect that your person was born around 1747 and you find a listing for a person with the same surname who was married in 1713 you probably haven't located the correct people yet. There are just too many years, 34, between the marriage date and your person's birth date. As a rule of thumb, people generally married when they were 20 years old and stopped having children when the mother was 45. This leaves about 25 years, at most, for bearing children. This is very valuable information that you should always keep in the back of your mind. Of course, a second marriage to a younger wife is always possible.

When you get stuck like this, information about your ancestor's brothers and sisters becomes very useful (see sibling searches). If you know that your person is the oldest of three other siblings, then it is very possible that the parents were married a year or two before your person's birth. Remember, you may not know if you have located every sibling. Even so, you can make intelligent guesses as to when the parents were married and when they were born.

With this in mind, you have to search through the indices checking out every name that makes sense with the years you have identified. This, of course, can be a very slow tedious job. Putting it bluntly, it is a lot of work and could take a lot of time. A fellow researcher once told me that it took him 17 years of research on one ancestor before he found that little piece of information that cracked it wide open for him. Hopefully you won't have to put quite this much effort into your family ancestry before you have success.

There is a little bit of good news but it may be small consolation when you are stuck on a particular family line. The number of states that were occupied before 1790 by early settlers was somewhat limited. As you might expect, that number is most probably 13, representing the original 13 colonies. There certainly were well established settlements, especially in the larger cities, but you must remember that for a majority of this time period there was not a formal government in place. The Declaration of Independence wasn't adopted until July 4, 1776, and Washington wasn't inaugurated as the country's first President until April 30, 1789. Most of the record keeping was left up to the cities and towns themselves. Massachusetts, for example, has published birth, marriage, and death records for many of its towns from 1690 to 1850. This is extremely valuable if your ancestors were from this state. If they were not, then you will have to contact the city clerk or library of the town and state you suspect your ancestor was from and check their records for the information you are looking for. It is unfortunate that none of the other states have as complete records as Massachusetts for the seventeen hundreds.

Trick #8

I highly recommend this next research technique whenever you reach a stumbling block on any ancestor. Putting it quite simply, when you have reached an impasse on a particular person and have spent days, weeks or even months on him/her, you should stop and do absolutely nothing! I mean stop researching completely on this ancestor. Go on to someone else for a few weeks or go on vacation somewhere so that you don't even think about this person for at least a month.

This at first may seem counterproductive but there really is a method to this technique. I have found in my own work that when you are buried knee-deep in all the papers, books, notes and scribblings, you could very well be overlooking or forgetting something very obvious or simple. It may be weeks or even months after you first start on an ancestor before you get to this point of making little or no progress. By then you probably will have forgotten something important that you may have already known. You need to try and step back from the reference books and get a different fresh viewpoint of the ancestor you are researching.

If you work on a different ancestor and make some real progress, when you do get back to your "dead end person," you will have a refreshed attitude with renewed determination for success. This boost in emotion is extremely important if you are to be successful. You might be very surprised to learn the things you overlooked or just didn't check the first time around.

Detailed Discussion of Resources

The discussions about the available resources is quite brief because all but three, compiled early settlers indices, compiled genealogies and special state censuses were discussed in previous chapters. A few general comments about the others here should be sufficient.

How you make use of and where to locate each resource is identical to that described in earlier chapters. The major difference, as I have already mentioned, is their limited availability and the decreased usefulness of their contents. Many towns never recorded any vital statistics at all in this time period. Many other records were lost in fires that occurred over the centuries. I can not even begin to tell you which towns in which states have fairly complete records and which ones do not. You will have to contact each and every municipal clerk's office or local library directly to discover which resources they have in their files. County historical societies and town and county historians can also help you here. They will know what records do exist for the area you are interested in.

Compiled Early Settlers Indicies

There exists several reference books which list the very earliest settlers of some cities, towns and states. Some of the books I am referring to were written by professional genealogists, historians and private citizens rather than state or federal employees. These books can be found in most of the larger genealogy and local history departments in public libraries. County historical societies also may have copies of these records.

The advantage that these resources offer is that they consist of a large number of alphabetized surnames. This allows you to go through several of these books fairly quickly checking for your ancestor. Of course, you may have to search through many of these books before you have success. This, however, should not take a great deal of time. What you may find is that you will run out of books to search through before you locate your person. Always remember when you are conducting a search to check all the possible alternate spellings of your person's surname.

If you still fail to locate your person, you must remember that this does not necessarily mean that he/she is not an early settler of that town. All it means is that your person is not listed in the books you checked. There may be books that your library does not have that could have your person listed or your person just wasn't important enough to be listed in any of these books. Many of them only contain biographies of the prominent people of the town. Either case is possible and it strictly depends upon where the research is being conducted.

Now, if you have already been in contact with the main library in the city and state you suspect your ancestor is from, and exhausted what books they have on their shelves, then you really may be out of luck. That is at least as far as this resource is concerned. I suggest trying other resources if this happens to you.

The types of information that this resource may contain is; a very brief description of where the person was from, family members including wife, where and when the person was born, occupation and places of residence. Some of these books do contain several generations of family information. Most of this genealogy information is contained in a separate section of town history reference books. Whoever first compiled and published a history of your town of interest, may have included genealogy information about the town's first settlers. You will probably have to contact a library in that town or county for this resource.

You must remember that you are looking for information that is 200 to 250 years old. At that time, the way of life and culture were quite different from today. What people valued then and considered important for official record keeping may not seem of such great importance today. It may benefit your research for this time period to check up on the lifestyles and ways of living for the area your ancestors are from. This will especially help you when you ask yourself the question "how did grandpa ancestor ever meet grandma ancestor and end up getting married?" This will greatly influence which resources in what towns make the most sense to search through first. This is important enough to be written down and tucked in your "how to use resources file" whenever you are conducting research in this time period.

Compiled Genealogies

These records are one of the most valuable resources that exists for conducting genealogical research in any time period. If you can find one of your ancestors in a previously compiled family history, you may be able to locate several generations of ancestors from this one resource. The key point here is to make the connection into one of these books. This leads me into the reason why I have put the discussion of this resource in this chapter.

As I just stated, for this resource to be useful, you have to be able to find one of your ancestors listed in one of these books. I have found that in order for this connection to be made you have to have your ancestor's lineage traced back several generations.

Most probably the person who compiled the family history you are interested in does not have your particular family line traced down to your generation. They published the information that pertained to their own lineage which more than likely is different from yours. If not, even better for you.

You may become excited when you find an 800 page family genealogy that shares the same surname as the person you are researching. But don't get too excited just yet because I've done it several times with nothing to show for that "great find." You may not locate your ancestor in the index and the reasons for this could be that there is absolutely no relationship between your family line and theirs, or there is a family connection but it won't become evident until you are able to trace your family line back another few generations.

This point needs to be stressed a little further. If at first you do not make the connection into one of these family genealogy books, you should remember to come back to them after you have located a few more generations of your particular family line. In fact you may want to come back and check in these books after each new ancestor you locate. Hopefully after a couple of tries you will be able to make the crucial connection.

Where you locate and how you use these books is fairly straightforward. Most local history and genealogy departments of the larger libraries will have somewhat of a collection on their shelves. The county and local historical societies should also have some family histories. These may be restricted to the people from that particular county and general locale however. The Library of Congress in 1972, 1977, 1981 and 1987 published listings of all the compiled family genealogies in their massive collection. You might be able to find some of the surnames you are researching in these listings. These books also tell you what other libraries around the country you can find the particular family genealogies you are interested in if you are not planning a trip to Washington, DC.

Family genealogy books are really quite simple to use once you find them. Most of them have an index of surnames in the back of the book that you can search through for your ancestor. If you go in with the frame of mind that actually locating your ancestor in one of these books is quite slim, then you won't be as let down as you might be if you think that this family history book you just found has all the answers you are looking for. This also enhances the excitement when you really do make a connection. Believe me, I know!

Special State Censuses

These censuses are not very numerous and were sparsely conducted before the first federal census of 1790. They were conducted by state and only 21 states conducted such censuses. The list below shows which states conducted censuses and the years they were conducted. For a more complete treatment of these special state censuses see the discussion found in *The Source*.

Connecticut: 1636, 1709, 1756, 1762, 1774

Delaware: 1665, 1667, 1669, 1670, 1671, 1672, 1675, 1676, 1677, 1678, 1680, 1681, 1693, 1696, 1697, 1776

Florida: 1783, 1786

Georgia: 1738, 1740, 1750, 1753, 1756

Illinois: 1787

Louisiana: 1699–1732, 1706, 1721, 1722, 1724, 1726, 1731, 1770–98, 1774

Maine: 1652, 1674, 1703, 1711, 1753

Maryland: 1683, 1701, 1704, 1708, 1710, 1712, 1748–1749, 1755, 1758, 1762, 1776, 1778

Massachusetts: 1754, 1764, 1779, 1783, 1785–86

Michigan: 1710–1830

Mississippi: 1774, 1788, 1789

Missouri: 1789

New Hampshire: 1633–99, 1732, 1735, 1767, 1773, 1774, 1775, 1786

New Jersey: 1693, 1726, 1737–38, 1745, 1772

New York: 1663, 1664, 1698, 1703, 1712–14, 1723, 1731, 1737, 1746, 1749, 1756, 1771

North Carolina: 1701, 1741–52, 1784, 1785, 1786, 1787

Pennsylvania: 1693, 1749, 1763–1807

Rhode Island: 1689, 1708, 1730, 1747, 1748–49, 1754, 1755, 1776, 1777, 1782

South Carolina: 1670, 1775, 1776

Vermont: 1623–25, 1634, 1699, 1701, 1703, 1779

Virginia: 1623–25, 1634, 1699, 1701, 1703, 1779

You can locate the special state censuses at most local history and genealogy departments in the larger public libraries. However, these censuses are not very common and you may find in your library only the censuses for the state in which the library is located. County historical societies may also have them in their files. Since these records are indexed alphabetically, it shouldn't take you too long to look up your ancestors to see if they are listed.

TOPICS:

the very earliest settlers and the arrival of the Pilgrims

helpful research tricks

AVAILABLE RESOURCES:

birth/marriage/death records   IGI

cemetery records   immigration indices

church records   land/mortgage records

city/town directories   military records

compiled early settlers indices   newspapers

• compiled genealogies   • ship passenger lists

compiled town histories   special state censuses

family Bibles   wills

• denotes the resources discussed in this chapter

1700 TO 1620

If you have successfully traced one or more of your family lines to this time period, the very earliest settlers and the arrival of the Pilgrims, then you deserve a firm congratulations on a job(s) well done! Your work isn't finished quite yet, but you can be assured that most of the hard work is behind you.

Of all the time periods I have discussed, I find this one to be the most exciting. If one of your family lines has survived to this point, then you could be in for some interesting and exciting discoveries. This is when you will learn what country your ancestors emigrated from, what ship they came over on, or maybe even which ancestors, if any, were Pilgrims who came over on the Mayflower in 1620. More probably you will learn that your ancestor(s) assisted in the founding of one of the very early settlements. One thing will most definitely be true when you complete your research in this time period. You will know who your immigrant ancestors are for each of your surviving family lines. When you know who these people are you will have achieved the goal you set for yourself when you started this project.

There are several reasons why this time period is my favorite to conduct research in. The first, as I mentioned, is the prospect of what you may learn about your immigrant ancestors. I learned that I had a great-great-great- . . . grandmother who was kidnapped by a tribe of Indians in the 1670s and forced to bare several children to the chief of the tribe. She was returned several years later to her own family. Although this information isn't the most pleasant to discover, it is interesting. Who knows what secrets about your ancestors lie waiting for you to discover.

Another reason why I like to conduct research in this time period is the small number of people who lived in America (excluding Native Americans) in the 17th century. When the 102 Pilgrims arrived at Province Town aboard the Mayflower on November 21, 1620, much to the surprise of many people including the author, they were not the first settlers to come to America although they were the first in New England. There were at least four settlements which predate the arrival of the Pilgrims. The Spaniards first arrived in 1565 and settled at St. Augustine Florida; the settlement at Jamestown, Virginia was started in May of 1607 by the English; Santa Fe, New Mexico was established in 1610 by Don Pedro de Peralta; and Bergen, New Jersey was settled by the Dutch in 1617 (Britannica 946).

Even with these settlements there were only 250,000 people (excluding Native Americans) living in America by 1700. At first this may sound like a lot of people, but actually it isn't. If you consider that these people were spread out among the 100+ towns that existed in the 1600s, you realize that each town on average may have had less than a thousand residents. This is a very manageable number of people to research on a town by town basis.

With these settlements predating the arrival of the Pilgrims, you may ask the question "why then do we recognize them and the Mayflower as the first settlers of America?." My feeling is that we recognize them as the first settlers in New England and assume that this means the first settlers everywhere. Now we know that this is not the case. I must say that of the settlements I have mentioned, the story of the Pilgrims is certainly the most entertaining.

A note of interest here about the word Pilgrim. The first settlers were not referred to by this term. In fact, they were originally called the Old Comers and then later they were known as the Forefathers. It wasn't until about 200 years after their arrival that the term Pilgrim was adopted. A manuscript of Governor William Bradford was discovered in which he refers to the "saints" who had left Holland as "pilgrimes." In 1820, Daniel Webster first used the phrase Pilgrim Fathers while speaking at a commemorative bicentennial celebration. The phrase caught on quickly and it became commonly used thereafter (Britannica 1006).

The third reason I enjoy researching in this time period is the superb availability of information on these early settlers. The people who immigrated to America during the 1600s were the founders of any and all towns and settlements that were started before 1700. These settlements have been researched and documented very well by hundreds of people over the past three and one half centuries. More attention has been given to these people simply because they are our founding fathers. There are several resources which list alphabetically thousands of people who immigrated before 1700. I have listed some of these in the bibliography under Immigration and Ship Passenger. (See Banks and Tepper).

There are also societies which require in their charter, that all members be descended from a particular group of people such as a Mayflower descendant. This particular genealogy society is a very exclusive and "prestigious" society as you can well imagine.

A final comment about the time period itself is needed here. You should remember that the way of life then differed significantly from today. A large percentage of the immigrants were not free men. You will find in the records, references to individuals (usually men) being granted freedom from the British Government. As the years passed you find fewer such references because eventually people were born with their freedom as an infant and didn't have to apply for it as an adult.

Detailed Discussion of Resources

I have only flagged two resources for discussion here and one of these, compiled genealogies, I discussed previously in the fourth chapter. The reason I treat it again here is explained below.

Before I discuss the resources for this time period in detail, I need to say a few words about them specifically. As I mentioned, there is a lot of information available on a very high percentage of the total number of people who were alive during this time period. So much so that I believe there is more information available per person for this time period than for any of those previously discussed. Since so few people lived and died before 1700, as I mentioned an estimated 250,000 living in America by 1700, all the research efforts to date for this time period have been directed toward these 250,000+ people. For comparison, consider the amount of information available between 1820 and 1900, but now you must weigh that against the number of people who lived during this period. The estimate for the American population in

1900 was slightly less than 76,000,000 people (Britannica 946). This is about 300 times the number of people that were living in America in 1700 (again excluding Native Americans). To maintain the same resource-to-people ratio that existed in the late 1600s, there would have to be 300 times as much information available in 1900 on these 76,000,000 people. Although this is impossible to accurately measure, in general this is certainly not the case.

The point I am trying to convey here is, for all intents and purposes, the only requirement necessary to be successful in this time period is that you are able to trace one or more of your family lines back to this time period. This, unfortunately, is something which you have absolutely no control over. If every one of your ancestors immigrated to America after 1860 for example, then obviously you will not be able to ever trace one of your own family lines to this exciting time period. The old saying "the one thing in life that you can never choose is your blood relations" certainly applies here!

Compiled Genealogies

Trick #9

When you finally get the chance to conduct research in this time period, you should pay more attention to this resource initially than any other. You could quite possibly save yourself some work if you are able to make the connection into a previously researched family history that shares the same surname as one of your ancestors. A high majority of these compiled genealogies start with the immigrant ancestor who more than likely immigrated in the 1600s. This increases the probability that you will be successful in locating your ancestor in one of these resources for this time period. I realize that I am really not telling you anything new here, but I do believe this resource just might help you the most with your research in this time period. If you need additional information about this resource refer to fourth chapter.

You must remember not to assume that just because you find information in a published book of some sort that all of the information you find is correct. You should always check what you find against other available resources. There is an added benefit that you might gain if you do some rechecking. You may learn something that is not contained in this resource. Sometimes the family line which you are interested in was not the line which the author put most of his focus on, so the information may be somewhat sketchy.

Ship Passenger Arrival Lists

This resource is very similar to Immigration Indices that were discussed in the fourth chapter with one minor difference. The ships that the people came over on were making their maiden voyages during this time and in some records the people are listed according to the ship name rather than the date. In addition to this, many of the ships made more than one voyage across the Atlantic Ocean over a ten or twenty year period. If you know the year of immigration and not the ship, you may have to look through several ship arrival lists before you find your immigrant. Conversely, you may know the ship your ancestor immigrated on but not the year, which may also require looking through several passenger arrival lists for the same ship but different voyages. Either one of these is probably equally possible and you will just have to check it out to learn which case applies to each of your ancestors.

There is always the possibility that you will not be able to locate your ancestor at all in any of these records. Your particular ancestor may not have been listed on the ship's log for any of a number of reasons, or the records that contain information about your ancestor, and others, are simply lost forever. Although this does happen on occasion, a majority of the time you will be successful in locating the immigration information you are seeking. If you need additional information about this type of resource, refer to the Immigration Indices discussion in the third chapter.

You will locate these records in most genealogy and local history departments of public libraries. Historical societies may also have copies of some of these resources. A simple telephone call to either or both of these places, local to you, will determine whether or not they have any of them in their files. A list of some of these indices is given in the bibliography.

MR. G

GENEALOGY IN THE YEAR 2010?

This final chapter is not related at all to the rest of the book nor to genealogical research. The reason I have included it here is that I hope you will find the subject matter interesting as it applies to family genealogy.

Will advancements in biological science make researching your family history impossible in the year 2010? Probably not for most of us but there will be an increasing number of people whose genealogy will be affected by this topic of discussion.

This question was made more difficult to answer on July 25, 1978, the day Louise Brown, the first test-tube baby, was born. To be more accurate, maybe I should have selected November 10, 1977, the day she was conceived. In either case, biologists and modern science have now provided us with alternate ways to have children in addition to "Mother Nature's original method." This is a little distressing to the genealogist because some very interesting and possibly unanswerable questions result.

Let me be a little more specific about what I mean. Every person that has ever lived was conceived from a single egg produced by a female, a single sperm cell produced by a male and carried for nine months, or so, by a female. These three elements must all work together in order for a child to be born. Therefore, genealogically speaking, each one of us truly has a biologically identifiable mother and father. Until about a decade ago, your biological mother and father were probably fairly easy to identify. There are, of course, some circumstances which could make identifying who these people are quite difficult; adoption, a person who had more than one spouse, or a woman who conceived via artificial insemination [AI]. These options have existed for hundreds of years and are just a few of the problems we genealogists have to deal with. With the terms mother and father defined as they apply to genealogy, let us explore what else technology has to offer.

Today it is possible to have either natural or a donor

substitute for each of the three elements, giving a total of eight possible methods of having a child. "Third party" mothers and fathers are possible via donations and more recently so are surrogate mothers. Surrogate mothers carry the fertilized egg to term, deliver the baby and then hand the child over to the awaiting parents. A very interesting case of surrogate motherhood which illustrates this point appeared in the newspaper a few years ago. The article stated that a woman in South Africa gave birth to her own triplet grandchildren! You can imagine the confusion these triplets will have when they attempt to fill in the "mother" information on their Pedigree Chart. Refer to the article in *TIME Magazine*, September 10, 1984, for a more complete discussion on this topic.

If your parents or maybe even grandparents were conceived using one of the AI methods, it may be difficult to confirm it through any type of formal records or documents. To be honest, I have never come across a single record which remotely suggested that the person I was researching was conceived via AI. You will probably have to check medical records and AI clinics for this information. If you do locate the right clinic, they probably won't share any information with you because of the donor's right to remain anonymous. This means, of course, that you will not be able to learn the surname or any of his or her family heritage!

In-vitro fertilization [IVF] offers additional options to the couple who wishes or needs to use an artificial method. In-vitro fertilization means that conception occurs artificially outside of the female's body. Since the successful birth of Louise Brown in 1978, there have been hundreds of children born via IVF. If one or more of these IVF children research their family history, who should they enter as their parents on the Pedigree Chart? The biological "bloodline" parent(s), or the parent(s) who raised them. For genealogical purposes the donor (biological) person(s) is the appropriate person(s) to list on the chart. However, since these IVF children have always considered the people who raised them to be their parents, the decision about which family history to research is clearly up to the individual. They always have the option of researching both family lines if they so choose!

There may be a middle ground for both the researcher and the clerks at the AI and IVF clinics. The laws which exist to protect the donor's identity and prohibit access by the offspring today, could be reformed to allow access after the donor has died. This would maintain complete privacy for the donor while they are alive and still inform the children born from their donation of their family heritage. If you think about it this could effect a large number of people. For example, it is entirely possible for a single male donor to give to a clinic dozens of times. This, of course, means that this one individual could be the biological father of dozens of children.

Access to these records will probably have to be decided by the courts. Considering that there are already some very interesting custody cases involving surrogate mothers and possession of "their" child, the next twenty years should reveal some very interesting "family" situations.

APPENDIX

AHNENTAFEL CHART

The Ahnentafel Chart is a condensed version of the Pedigree Chart in which only the names of the people, your ancestors, are listed. In case you are wondering, Ahnentafel is a German word meaning "ancestor table."

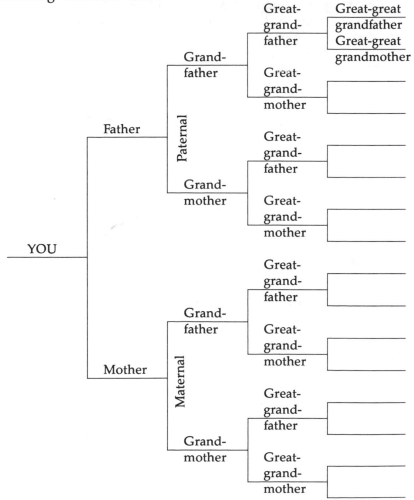

DIRECT ANCESTOR TABLE

The Direct Ancestor Table is simply a listing of the multiples of the number 2. Starting with yourself as generation #1, your parents (2 people) as generation #2, your grandparents (4 people) as generation #3 and so forth, higher generations of people are listed in first column with their associated multiple of two listed in the third column. The number of years per generation is estimated to be 28 and is given in the second column. This was arrived at from calculating the average number of years per generation for several sets of 12 generation lineages. The fourth column lists the sum of all of the people up to and including that generation.

Gen.	# Years	# People	Sum	Comment
1	28	1	1	Yourself
2	56	2	3	Parents
3	84	4	7	Grandparents
4	112	8	15	
5	140	16	31	
.	.	.	.	
9	252	256	511	
10	280	512	1023	
11	308	1024	2047	
12	336	2048	4095	Pilgrims—1620
13	364	4096	8191	
14	392	8192	16383	
15	420	16384	32767	
.	.	.	.	
19	532	262144	524287	
20	560	524288	1048575	
21	588	1048576	2097151	
22	616	2097152	4194303	
23	644	4194304	8388607	
24	672	8388608	16777215	
.	.	.	.	
34	952	8589934592	17179869183	1066–William the Conquerer
.	.	.		
71	1988	1180000000000000000000		Birth of Christ

CHASE FAMILY DESCENDANT CHART

Generations of descent are numbered from the earliest know ancestor:

William Chase
  1. William Chase
    2. John Chase
      3. Thomas Chase
        4. Richard Chase
          5. John Chase
            6. John Chase
              7. Neri Chase
                8. Andrew Jackson Chase
                  9. Reuben Willis Chase
                    10. Rolfe Baker Chase
                      11. Rolfe Baker Chase, Jr.
                      11. Bradford Savage Chase
                        12. Scott Bradford Chase
                          13. Patrick Douglas Chase
                        12. Gary Dana Chase
                        12. Kristi Ann Chase
                        12. Bryan Mark Chase
                      11. Deborah Gale Chase
                    10. Gardener Wendell Chase

PEDIGREE CHART

DATE February 1982

NAME OF PERSON SUBMITTING CHART
Scott B. Chase

STREET ADDRESS

CITY   STATE

NO. 1 ON THIS CHART IS
THE SAME PERSON AS NO.

ON CHART NO.

1 Scott Bradford Chase
BORN March 11 1958
WHEN Northampton MA
WHEN MARRIED 8/2 1986
DIED
WHERE

Md: Cathy Rowena Stuart

NAME OF HUSBAND OR WIFE

Md: Rochester NY

GIVE HERE NAME OF RECORD OR
BOOK WHERE THIS INFORMATION
WAS OBTAINED. REFER TO NAMES
BY NUMBER.

2 Bradford Savage Chase
BORN July 29 1934
WHERE Taunton MA
WHEN MARRIED 6/8 1957
DIED
WHERE

Md: Rochester NY

3 Ann Elizabeth Persse
BORN March 27 1936
WHERE Syracuse NY
DIED
WHERE

4 Rolfe Baker Chase
BORN August 31 1908
WHERE Taunton MA
WHEN MARRIED 10/5 1929
DIED April 3 1986
WHERE Taunton MA

Md: Taunton MA

5 Ada Mabel VanVranken
BORN July 27 1906
WHERE Taunton MA
DIED
WHERE

Md: Rochester NY

6 Harriet Elizabeth Bruce
BORN September 9 1908
WHERE Rochester NY
WHEN MARRIED 6/21 1934
DIED
WHERE

7 Ernest Howard Persse
BORN August 2 1910
WHERE Syracuse NY
DIED June 20 1969
WHERE Rochester NY

8 Reuben Willis Chase
BORN April 24 1882
WHERE Harwich MA
WHEN MARRIED 10/5 1905
DIED August 30 1959
WHERE Taunton MA

9 Ethel Irene Savage
BORN January 19 1882
WHERE Wakefield MA
DIED June 14 1953
WHERE Lakeville MA

10 Howard VanVranken

11 Mabel Dutcher
BORN November 20 1878
WHERE Albany NY
DIED July 26 1912
WHERE Taunton MA

12 Sara Belle Emmons

13 Robert Malcolm Bruce
BORN January 15 1879
WHERE Buffalo NY
DIED June 8 1962
WHERE Rochester NY

14 Bertha Evangeline Crowell

15 Fred Blakeney Persse
BORN January 3 1880
WHERE Johnstown NY
DIED May 31 1939
WHERE Buffalo NY

16 Andrew Jackson Chase
CHART NO. 1

17 Eunisa Baker
ABOVE NAME CONTINUED ON CHART 2

18 William Frank Savage
ABOVE NAME CONTINUED ON CHART 3

19 Augusta Ayre Brown
ABOVE NAME CONTINUED ON CHART 4

20 Francis Edward VanVranken
ABOVE NAME CONTINUED ON CHART 5

21 Martha Jane Stevens
ABOVE NAME CONTINUED ON CHART 6

22 William Wallace Dutcher
ABOVE NAME CONTINUED ON CHART 7

23 Sarah Elizabeth Millett
ABOVE NAME CONTINUED ON CHART 8

24 Harriet Frances Wells
ABOVE NAME CONTINUED ON CHART 9

25 William Alva Emmons
ABOVE NAME CONTINUED ON CHART 10

26 Alice Maria Humphryes
ABOVE NAME CONTINUED ON CHART 11

27 Robert Maxwell Bruce
ABOVE NAME CONTINUED ON CHART 12

28 Ursula Wardwell
ABOVE NAME CONTINUED ON CHART 13

29 Samuel E. Crowell
ABOVE NAME CONTINUED ON CHART 14

30 Alida Jane Heagel
ABOVE NAME CONTINUED ON CHART 15

31 Burton Persse
ABOVE NAME CONTINUED ON CHART 16

Born detail notes:
- **16** WHERE Taunton MA
- **17** WHERE Harwich MA
- **18** DIED 10/5 1959
- **21** BORN July 8 1877, WHERE Beverly MA, WHEN MARRIED 1/2 1898, DIED September 3 1939
- **25** BORN April 3 1879, WHERE Buffalo NY, WHEN MARRIED 6/20 1905
- **26** DIED October 28 1961, WHERE Orlando FL
- **27** BORN January 15 1879, WHERE Buffalo NY, DIED June 8 1962, WHERE Rochester NY
- **28** WHERE Rochester NY
- **29** BORN July 21 1874, WHERE Lynn MA, WHEN MARRIED 10/26 1904, DIED May 7 1948, WHERE Buffalo NY

PEDIGREE CHART

DATE _____
Scott B. Chase
NAME OF PERSON SUBMITTING CHART

STREET ADDRESS _____

CITY _____   STATE _____

NO. 1 ON THIS CHART IS ____18____
THE SAME PERSON AS NO. ____I____

ON CHART NO. ____I____

16 William Savage

8 John Savage (Rev. War) (bp)
BORN September 30 1744
WHERE Marblehead MA
DIED
WHEN MARRIED 12/14 1769
WHERE

17 Charity Tucker
ABOVE NAME CONTINUED ON CHART 301

18
ABOVE NAME CONTINUED ON CHART 302

9 Mary Jackson
BORN
WHERE
DIED
WHERE

19
ABOVE NAME CONTINUED ON CHART 303

4 William Savage **
BORN Greenfield NH 1784
WHERE
WHEN MARRIED 11/11 1813
DIED 1862
WHERE

10 Joseph Hodge
BORN
WHERE
DIED
WHERE

20
ABOVE NAME CONTINUED ON CHART 304

21
ABOVE NAME CONTINUED ON CHART 305

2 Joseph Gardner Savage
BORN September 17 1825
WHERE Greenfield NH
WHEN MARRIED
DIED October 25 1898 **
WHERE Wakefield MA **

5 Joanna Hodge (Hogg–Irish)
BORN 1790 *
**WHERE Jaffrey NH
DIED 1872
WHERE

22 Richard Alexander
ABOVE NAME CONTINUED ON CHART 306

11 Elizabeth Alexander
BORN December 13 1757
WHERE Marlborough MA
DIED November 13 1841
WHERE

23 Jerusha
ABOVE NAME CONTINUED ON CHART 307

24 Esther Lewis
ABOVE NAME CONTINUED ON CHART 308

1 William Frank Savage **Md: Wakefield MA
BORN December 27 1855
WHERE Wakefield MA
WHEN MARRIED 1879
DIED May 9 1932
WHERE Taunton MA

12 (Lewis) Esther Willoughby
BORN March 19 1810/19
WHERE Milford NH
WHEN MARRIED 1831
DIED November 16 1874
WHERE Milford NH

25 Abijah Wood
ABOVE NAME CONTINUED ON CHART 309

13 Polly (Mary) Wood
BORN 1774
WHERE Hollis NH
WHEN MARRIED 3/17 1796
WHERE
DIED
WHERE

26 Hannah Bates
ABOVE NAME CONTINUED ON CHART 310

27 Jonas Willoughby
ABOVE NAME CONTINUED ON CHART 311

6 David Willoughby
BORN April 15 1851
WHERE Milford NH
WHEN MARRIED
DIED April 4 1770
WHERE Hollis NH

28 Phebe Pierce
ABOVE NAME CONTINUED ON CHART 312

3 Harriet Peacock
BORN November 23 1836/5 **
WHERE Hollis NH **
WHEN MARRIED
DIED January 18 1883 **
WHERE Milford NH **

14 Elizabeth Foster
BORN 1777
WHERE Milford NH
WHEN MARRIED
DIED April 17 1837
WHERE Milford NH

29 Edward Foster
ABOVE NAME CONTINUED ON CHART 313

30 Abigail
ABOVE NAME CONTINUED ON CHART 314

7 Robert Peacock
BORN February 16 1809
WHERE Milford NH
WHEN MARRIED 1798
DIED April 21 1839/8
WHERE Milford NH

15 Daniel Peacock
BORN September 12 1776
WHERE Amherst NH
DIED 1820
WHERE Amherst NH

31 William Peacock
ABOVE NAME CONTINUED ON CHART 315

16 ...
WHERE Lempster
ABOVE NAME CONTINUED ON CHART 316

NAME OF HUSBAND OR WIFE
Augusta Ayre Brown

GIVE HERE NAME OF RECORD OR
BOOK WHERE THIS INFORMATION
WAS OBTAINED. REFER TO NAMES
BY NUMBER.

** signifies unconfirmed
information
bp baptized

PEDIGREE CHART

DATE _____

Scott B. Chase
NAME OF PERSON SUBMITTING CHART

STREET ADDRESS _____

CITY _____ STATE _____

NO. 1 ON THIS CHART IS __I__
THE SAME PERSON AS NO. __31__

ON CHART NO. __I__

GIVE HERE NAME OF RECORD OR
BOOK WHERE THIS INFORMATION
WAS OBTAINED. REFER TO NAMES
BY NUMBER.

CHART NO. 16

1 Burton Persse
BORN November 23 1841
WHERE Johnstown NY
WHEN MARRIED
DIED November 19 1884
WHERE Fort Hunter NY

NAME OF HUSBAND OR WIFE
Alida Jane Heagel

Md: Johnstown NY

2 Theophillus Blakeney Persse
BORN March 27 1806
WHERE Galway Ireland
WHEN MARRIED 2/10 1829
DIED December 13 1880
WHERE Johnstown NY

3 Mary Anne Edwards
BORN December 13 1806
WHERE Johnstown NY
DIED April 29 1883
WHERE Johnstown NY

4 Henry Stratford Persse
BORN Ireland
WHERE
WHEN MARRIED
DIED October 23 1833
WHERE New Castle
        Galway Ireland

5 Anne Sadleir
BORN
WHERE
DIED
WHERE

6 John Edwards
BORN
WHERE
WHEN MARRIED 3/18 1802
DIED December 28 1850
WHERE

7 Margaret Yanney
BORN November 13 1776
WHERE NY
DIED
WHERE NY

8 William Persse
BORN 1728
WHERE Roxborough Ire.
WHEN MARRIED (about) 1750
DIED 1802
WHERE Ireland

9 Sarah Blakeney
BORN Ireland
WHERE
DIED 1792
WHERE Ireland

10 Thomas Sadlier
BORN
WHERE MARRIED
DIED
WHERE

11
BORN
WHERE
DIED
WHERE

12 Talmadge Edwards
BORN 1747
WHERE
WHEN MARRIED
DIED 1780
WHERE NY

13 Mary Shearman
BORN December 4 1751
WHERE
DIED April 10 1815
WHERE Johnstown NY

14 Henry Yauney
BORN September 18 1746
WHERE
WHEN MARRIED 1/20 1776
DIED 1830
WHERE

15 Eliz. Margaret Cline
BORN June 10 1756
WHERE Johnstown NY
DIED
WHERE

16 Robert Persse

#	Name	ABOVE NAME CONTINUED ON CHART
16	Robert Persse	1601
17	Elizabeth Parsons	1602
18	Col. John Blakeney	1603
19	Grace Persse	1604
20	Richard Sadlier	1605
21		
22		
23		
24		
25		
26	Margaret Knowles	1611
27	Ezekiel Shearman	1612
28	Christian Yauney	1613
29	Susanah Boshart	1614
30	Philip Henry Cline	1615
31		1616

PEDIGREE CHART

DATE _____
NAME OF PERSON SUBMITTING CHART
Scott B. Chase

STREET ADDRESS

CITY _____ STATE _____

NO. 1 ON THIS CHART IS 29
THE SAME PERSON AS NO. _____

ON CHART NO. 3

** signifies unconfirmed
information
bur buried

GIVE HERE NAME OF RECORD OR
BOOK WHERE THIS INFORMATION
WAS OBTAINED. REFER TO NAMES
BY NUMBER.

1
Edward Foster
BORN April 3 1747
WHERE Chelmsford MA
WHEN MARRIED 1/23 1772
DIED April 3 1807
** WHERE Milford NH

Md: Chelmsford
MA

2
William Foster
BORN November 11 1716
WHERE Chelmsford MA
WHEN MARRIED 9/15 1744
DIED March 12 1786
WHERE Chelmsford MA

Md: Dracut MA

3
Hannah Colburn
BORN March 22 1724
WHERE Dracut MA
DIED(bur) July 4 1795
WHERE Chelmsford MA

NAME OF HUSBAND OR WIFE
Phebe Pierce

4
Edward Foster
BORN January 29 1689
WHERE
WHEN MARRIED
DIED
WHERE
**

5
Remembrance
BORN
WHERE
DIED
WHERE

6
Mercy Varnum
BORN April 17 1702
WHERE Dracut MA
WHEN MARRIED 12/9 1722
DIED 1785
WHERE

Md: Dracut MA

7
Aaron Colburn
BORN
WHERE
DIED February 24 1745
WHERE Dracut MA

8
Samuel Foster
BORN
WHERE
WHEN MARRIED
DIED
WHERE

9
Sarah
BORN
WHERE
DIED
WHERE

10
BORN
WHERE
WHEN MARRIED
DIED
WHERE

11
BORN
WHERE
DIED
WHERE

12
Joanna Jewett
BORN May 8 1677
WHERE Ipswich MA
WHEN MARRIED 11/10 1697
DIED April 6 1753
WHERE Dracut MA
Thomas Varnum

13
Samuel Varnum
BORN November 19 166
WHERE Ipswich MA
DIED September 7 1739
WHERE Dracut MA

14
BORN
WHERE
WHEN MARRIED
DIED
WHERE

---

16 _____ ABOVE NAME CONTINUED ON CHART

17 _____ ABOVE NAME CONTINUED ON CHART

18 _____ ABOVE NAME CONTINUED ON CHART

19 _____ ABOVE NAME CONTINUED ON CHART

20 _____ ABOVE NAME CONTINUED ON CHART

21 _____ ABOVE NAME CONTINUED ON CHART

22 _____ ABOVE NAME CONTINUED ON CHART

23 _____ ABOVE NAME CONTINUED ON CHART

24 Exercise Pierce _____ ABOVE NAME CONTINUED ON CHART 31409

25 Nehemiah Jewett _____ ABOVE NAME CONTINUED ON CHART 31410

26 Sarah Langton _____ ABOVE NAME CONTINUED ON CHART 31411

27 Samuel Varnum _____ ABOVE NAME CONTINUED ON CHART 31412

28 _____ ABOVE NAME CONTINUED ON CHART

29 _____ ABOVE NAME CONTINUED ON CHART

30 _____ ABOVE NAME CONTINUED ON CHART

31 _____ ABOVE NAME CONTINUED ON CHART

PEDIGREE CHART

CHART NO. 31412

DATE _____
Scott B. Chase
NAME OF PERSON SUBMITTING CHART

STREET ADDRESS _____

CITY _____ STATE _____

NO. 1 ON THIS CHART IS
THE SAME PERSON AS NO. 27

ON CHART NO. 314

1 Samuel Varnum
BORN 1619
WHERE England
WHEN MARRIED 1645
DIED after 1702
WHERE

NAME OF HUSBAND OR WIFE
Sarah Langton

GIVE HERE NAME OF RECORD OR
BOOK WHERE THIS INFORMATION
WAS OBTAINED. REFER TO NAMES
BY NUMBER.

2 George Varnum
BORN
WHERE England
WHEN MARRIED
DIED 1649
WHERE Ipswich MA

3 Hannah
BORN
WHERE England
DIED
WHERE

4
BORN
WHERE
WHEN MARRIED
DIED
WHERE

5
BORN
WHERE
DIED
WHERE

6
BORN
WHERE
WHEN MARRIED
DIED
WHERE

7
BORN
WHERE
DIED
WHERE

8
BORN
WHERE
WHEN MARRIED
DIED
WHERE

9
BORN
WHERE
DIED
WHERE

10
BORN
WHERE
WHEN MARRIED
DIED
WHERE

11
BORN
WHERE
DIED
WHERE

12
BORN
WHERE
WHEN MARRIED
DIED
WHERE

13
BORN
WHERE
DIED
WHERE

14
BORN
WHERE
WHEN MARRIED
DIED
WHERE

15
BORN
WHERE
DIED
WHERE

16 ABOVE NAME CONTINUED ON CHART _____

17 ABOVE NAME CONTINUED ON CHART _____

18 ABOVE NAME CONTINUED ON CHART _____

19 ABOVE NAME CONTINUED ON CHART _____

20 ABOVE NAME CONTINUED ON CHART _____

21 ABOVE NAME CONTINUED ON CHART _____

22 ABOVE NAME CONTINUED ON CHART _____

23 ABOVE NAME CONTINUED ON CHART _____

24 ABOVE NAME CONTINUED ON CHART _____

25 ABOVE NAME CONTINUED ON CHART _____

26 ABOVE NAME CONTINUED ON CHART _____

27 ABOVE NAME CONTINUED ON CHART _____

28 ABOVE NAME CONTINUED ON CHART _____

29 ABOVE NAME CONTINUED ON CHART _____

30 ABOVE NAME CONTINUED ON CHART _____

31 ABOVE NAME CONTINUED ON CHART _____

PEDIGREE CHART

DATE _____

NAME OF PERSON SUBMITTING CHART _____

STREET ADDRESS _____

CITY _____ STATE _____

NO. 1 ON THIS CHART IS
THE SAME PERSON AS NO. _____

ON CHART NO. _____

1
NAME OF HUSBAND OR WIFE
BORN
WHERE
WHEN MARRIED
DIED
WHERE

GIVE HERE NAME OF RECORD OR
BOOK WHERE THIS INFORMATION
WAS OBTAINED. REFER TO NAMES
BY NUMBER.

2
BORN
WHERE
WHEN MARRIED
DIED
WHERE

3
BORN
WHERE
DIED
WHERE

4
BORN
WHERE
WHEN MARRIED
DIED
WHERE

5
BORN
WHERE
DIED
WHERE

6
BORN
WHERE
WHEN MARRIED
DIED
WHERE

7
BORN
WHERE
DIED
WHERE

8
BORN
WHERE
WHEN MARRIED
DIED
WHERE

9
BORN
WHERE
DIED
WHERE

10
BORN
WHERE
WHEN MARRIED
DIED
WHERE

11
BORN
WHERE
DIED
WHERE

12
BORN
WHERE
WHEN MARRIED
DIED
WHERE

13
BORN
WHERE
DIED
WHERE

14
BORN
WHERE
WHEN MARRIED
DIED
WHERE

15
BORN
WHERE
DIED
WHERE

CHART NO _____

16 _____ ABOVE NAME CONTINUED ON CHART

17 _____ ABOVE NAME CONTINUED ON CHART

18 _____ ABOVE NAME CONTINUED ON CHART

19 _____ ABOVE NAME CONTINUED ON CHART

20 _____ ABOVE NAME CONTINUED ON CHART

21 _____ ABOVE NAME CONTINUED ON CHART

22 _____ ABOVE NAME CONTINUED ON CHART

23 _____ ABOVE NAME CONTINUED ON CHART

24 _____ ABOVE NAME CONTINUED ON CHART

25 _____ ABOVE NAME CONTINUED ON CHART

26 _____ ABOVE NAME CONTINUED ON CHART

27 _____ ABOVE NAME CONTINUED ON CHART

28 _____ ABOVE NAME CONTINUED ON CHART

29 _____ ABOVE NAME CONTINUED ON CHART

30 _____ ABOVE NAME CONTINUED ON CHART

31 _____ ABOVE NAME CONTINUED ON CHART

FAMILY GROUP No. _____

Husband's Full Name Bradford Savage Chase

This Information Obtained From:	Husband's Data	Day	Month	Year	City, Town or Place	County or Province, etc.	State or Country	Add. Info. on Husband
personal	Birth	29	7	1934	Taunton		MA	
interviews	Chr'nd							
	Mar.	8	6	1957	Rochester		NY	
	Death							
	Burial							

Places of Residence

Occupation _____ Church Affiliation Protestant Military Rec.

Other wives, if any. No. (1) (2) etc. Make separate sheet for each mar.

His Father Rolfe Baker   Mother's Maiden Name Ada Mabel VanVranken

Wife's Full Maiden Name Ann Elizabeth Persse

	Wife's Data	Day	Month	Year	City, Town or Place	County or Province, etc.	State or Country	Add. Info. on Wife
	Birth	27	3	1936	Syracuse		NY	
	Chr'nd							
	Death							
	Burial							

Compiler Scott Chase

Address

City, State

Date 10/9 1987

Places of Residence

Occupation if other than Housewife Teacher Church Affiliation Protestant

Other husbands, if any. No. (1) (2) etc. Make separate sheet for each that.

Her Father Ernest Howard   Mother's Maiden Name Harriet E. Bruce

Sex	Children's Names in Full (Arrange in order of birth)	Children's Data	Day	Month	Year	City, Town or Place	County or Province, etc.	State or Country	Add. Info. on Children
M	1 Scott Bradford / Full Name of Spouse* / Cathy Rowena Stuart	Birth	11	3	1958	Northampton		MA	
		Mar.	2	8	1986	Rochester	Monroe	NY	
		Death							
		Burial							
M	2 Gary Dana / Full Name of Spouse*	Birth	23	2	1960	Lansing		MI	
		Mar.							
		Death							
		Burial							
F	3 Kristi Ann / Full Name of Spouse* / James J. McKeever	Birth	19	11	1961	Sharon		PA	
		Mar.	8	6	1985	Enfield		CT	
		Death							
		Burial							
M	4 Bryan Mark / Full Name of Spouse*	Birth	15	6	1967	Springfield		MA	
		Mar.							
		Death							
		Burial							
	5 / Full Name of Spouse*	Birth							
		Mar.							
		Death							
		Burial							
	6 / Full Name of Spouse*	Birth							
		Mar.							
		Death							
		Burial							
	7 / Full Name of Spouse*	Birth							
		Mar.							
		Death							
		Burial							
	8 / Full Name of Spouse*	Birth							
		Mar.							
		Death							
		Burial							
	9 / Full Name of Spouse*	Birth							
		Mar.							
		Death							
		Burial							
	10 / Full Name of Spouse*	Birth							
		Mar.							
		Death							
		Burial							

*If married more than once No. each mar. (1) (2) etc. and list in "Add. Info. on children" column. Use reverse side for additional children, other notes, references or information.

FAMILY GROUP No. _____

Husband's Full Name

This Information Obtained From:

Husband's Data	Day Month Year	City, Town or Place	County or Province, etc.	State or Country	Add. Info. on Husband
Birth					
Chr'nd					
Mar.					
Death					
Burial					

Places of Residence

Occupation _____ Church Affiliation _____ Military Rec.

Other wives, if any. No. (1) (2) etc.
Make separate sheet for each mar.

His Father _____ Mother's Maiden Name

Wife's Full Maiden Name

Wife's Data	Day Month Year	City, Town or Place	County or Province, etc.	State or Country	Add. Info. on Wife
Birth					
Chr'nd					
Death					
Burial					

Compiler

Address

City, State

Date

Places of Residence

Occupation if other than Housewife _____ Church Affiliation

Other husbands, if any. No. (1) (2) etc.
Make separate sheet for each mar.

Her Father _____ Mother's Maiden Name

Sex	Children's Names in Full (Arrange in order of birth)	Children's Data	Day Month Year	City, Town or Place	County or Province, etc.	State or Country	Add. Info. on Children
	1 _____ Full Name of Spouse*	Birth Mar. Death Burial					
	2 _____ Full Name of Spouse*	Birth Mar. Death Burial					
	3 _____ Full Name of Spouse*	Birth Mar. Death Burial					
	4 _____ Full Name of Spouse*	Birth Mar. Death Burial					
	5 _____ Full Name of Spouse*	Birth Mar. Death Burial					
	6 _____ Full Name of Spouse*	Birth Mar. Death Burial					
	7 _____ Full Name of Spouse*	Birth Mar. Death Burial					
	8 _____ Full Name of Spouse*	Birth Mar. Death Burial					
	9 _____ Full Name of Spouse*	Birth Mar. Death Burial					
	10 _____ Full Name of Spouse*	Birth Mar. Death Burial					

*If married more than once No. each mar. (1) (2) etc. and list in "Add. info. on children" column. Use reverse side for additional children, other notes, references or information.

CHILDREN CONTINUATION SHEET for FAMILY GROUP No. ___

Form A11 Copyright 1962 by The Everton Publishers, Inc., P.O. Box 368, Logan, Utah. Publishers of THE GENEALOGICAL HELPER. Send for a free catalogue with lists and full descriptions of many genealogical aids.

Husband's full name_____

Wife's full maiden name_____

Sex	Children's Names in Full (Arrange in order of birth)	Children's Data	Day Month Year	City, Town or Place	County or Province, etc.	State or Country	Add. Info. on Children
	No.__	Birth					
		Mar.					
	Full Name of Spouse	Death					
		Burial					
	No.__	Birth					
		Mar.					
	Full Name of Spouse	Death					
		Burial					
	No.__	Birth					
		Mar.					
	Full Name of Spouse	Death					
		Burial					
	No.__	Birth					
		Mar.					
	Full Name of Spouse	Death					
		Burial					
	No.__	Birth					
		Mar.					
	Full Name of Spouse	Death					
		Burial					
	No.__	Birth					
		Mar.					
	Full Name of Spouse	Death					
		Burial					
	No.__	Birth					
		Mar.					
	Full Name of Spouse	Death					
		Burial					
	No.__	Birth					
		Mar.					
	Full Name of Spouse	Death					
		Burial					
	No.__	Birth					
		Mar.					
	Full Name of Spouse	Death					
		Burial					
	No.__	Birth					
		Mar.					
	Full Name of Spouse	Death					
		Burial					
	No.__	Birth					
		Mar.					
	Full Name of Spouse	Death					
		Burial					
	No.__	Birth					
		Mar.					
	Full Name of Spouse	Death					
		Burial					
	No.__	Birth					
		Mar.					
	Full Name of Spouse	Death					
		Burial					
	No.__	Birth					
		Mar.					
	Full Name of Spouse	Death					
		Burial					

NOTE TAKING FORM

Bradford Savage Chase
Born: July 29 1934   At: Taunton MA   Died:
Father:Rolfe Baker Chase   At:
Married:Ann Elizabeth Persse When: June 8 1957   Where: Rochester NY
Born: March 27 1936   At: Syracuse NY   Died:
Father: Ernest Howard Persse   At:
Children: Born: At: Died:
     Scott Bradford   3/11 1958   Northampton MA
     Gary Dana   2/23 1960   Lansing MI
     Kristi Ann   11/19 1961   Sharon PA
     Bryan Mark   6/15 1967   Springfield MA

Scott Bradford Chase
Born: March 11 1958   At: Northampton MA   Died:
Father:Bradford Savage Chase   At:
Married: Cathy Rowena Stuart When: August 2 1986 Where: Rochester NY
Born: March 17 1958   At: Rochester NY   Died:
Father:Douglas Eugene Stuart   At:
Children: Born: At: Died:
     Patrick Douglas 8/14 1988 Rochester NY

Kristi Ann Chase
Born: November 19 1961   At: Sharon PA   Died:
Father: Bradford Savage Chase   At:
Married: James Joseph McKeever When: June 8 1985 Where: Enfield CT
Born: February 9 1961   At: Bronx NY   Died:
Father: Joseph Patrick McKeever   At:
Children: Born: At: Died:
     Erica Ann   1/27 1986 San Francisco CA

NOTE TAKING FORM

Born: At: Died:
Father: At:
Married: When: Where:
Born: At: Died:
Father: At:
Children: Born: At: Died:

Born: At: Died:
Father: At:
Married: When: Where:
Born: At: Died:
Father: At:
Children: Born: At: Died:

Born: At: Died:
Father: At:
Married: When: Where:
Born: At: Died:
Father: At:
Children: Born: At: Died:

BIBLIOGRAPHY

There are hundreds of books published that discuss the topic of genealogical research and its associated reference materials. I have listed what I feel is a few of the more valuable references based on their informational content. The books are separated into categories according to their subject matter.

General

Eakle, A., and J. Cerny, ed. *The SOURCE: A Guidebook of American Genealogy.* Salt Lake City: Ancestry, Inc., 1984.

Kaminkow, M. J., ed. *Genealogies in the Library of Congress; A Bibliography.* vols. 1 & 2. Baltimore: Magna Carta Book Co., 1972.

Kaminkow, M. J., ed. *Genealogies in the Library of Congress: A Bibliography Supplement 1972–1976.* Baltimore: Magna Carta Book Co., 1977.

Kaminkow, M. J., ed. *A Compliment to Genealogies in the Library of Congress.* Baltimore: Magna Carta Book Co., 1981.

Kaminkow, M. J., ed. *Genealogies in the Library of Congress: A Bibliography Second Supplement 1976–1986.* Baltimore: Magna Carta, 1987.

Smith, B. P. *Directory: Historical Agencies in North America.* 13th ed. Nashville: American Association for State and Local History, 1986.

The American Association of Museums. *The Official Museum Directory—1990.* Wilmette, IL: National Register, 1989.

The Genealogical Department of The Church of Jesus Christ of Latter-day Saints. *The International Genealogical Index* (IGI). Salt Lake City: Corporation of the President of The Church of Jesus Christ of Latter-day Saints, 1983.

How-To

American Genealogy Research Institute Staff. *How To Trace Your Family Tree: A Complete and Easy to Understand Guide for the Beginner.* New York: Doubleday, 1975.

Beard, T. F., and D. Demong. *How to Find Your Family Roots.* New York: McGraw-Hill, 1977.

Dixon, J. T., and D. D. Flack. *Preserving Your Past: A Painless Guide to*

Writing Your Autobiography and Family History. New York: Doubleday, 1977.

Doane, G. H., and J. B. Bell. *Searching for Your Ancestors: The How and Why of Genealogy.* 5th ed. Minneapolis: University of Minnesota, 1980.

Everton, G. B. *The Handy Book for Genealogists.* 6th ed. Logan, UT: Everton Publishers, 1971.

Greenwood, V. D. *The Researchers Guide to American Genealogy.* 2nd Edition, Baltimore: Genealogical Publishing Co, 1990.

Kirkham, E. K. *Simplified Genealogy for Americans.* Salt Lake City: Deseret Book, 1973.

Lichtman, A. J. *Your Family History.* 1st ed. New York: Vintage Books, 1978.

Stetson, O. F. *The Art of Ancestor Hunting: A Guide to Ancestral Research and Genealogy.* 4th print. New York: Stephen Daye, 1965.

Royalty

D'Angerville, H. H., Count, ed. *Living Descendants of Blood Royal (In America).* vols. 1 & 2. London: World Nobility and Peerage, 1961.

Kimber, E., and R. Johnson. *The Baronetage of England: Containing A Genealogy and Historical Account of all the English Baronets.* vols. 1 & 2. London. 1771.

Montague-Smith, P., ed. *Debrett's Peerage and Baronetage with Her Majesty's Royal Warrant Holders 1976.* London: The Viking, 1977.

Searle, W. G. *Anglo-Saxon Bishops, Kings and Nobles.* Cambridge, MA: Cambridge at the University, 1899.

Burke's

Burke, J. *A Genealogical and Heraldic History of the Commoners of Great Britain and Ireland.* vols. 1–4 London: Henry Colburn, 1836.

Burke, B., Sir. *Burke's Genealogical and Heraldic History of the Landed Gentry: Including American Families with British Ancestry.* London: Burke's Peerage, 1939.

Pine, L. G., ed. *Burke's Genealogical and Heraldic History of the Landed Gentry of Ireland.* 4th ed. London: Burke's Peerage, 1958.

Tepper, M., ed. *Burke's American Families with British Ancestry: The Lineages of 1000 Families of British Origin Now Resident in the USA.* Baltimore: Genealogical Publishing Co., 1975.

Townend, P., ed. *Burke's Genealogy and Heraldic History of the Landed Gentry.* 18th ed. London: Burke's Peerage, 1965.

Immigration and Ship Passenger

Banks, C. E. *Topographical Dictionary of 2885 English Emigrants to New England 1620–1650*. Baltimore: Southern Book, 1957.

Bolton, E. S. *Immigrants to New England 1700–1775*. Boston: The Essex Institute, 1931.

Boyer, C. 3rd., ed. *Ship Passenger Lists: National and New England (1600–1825)*. Newhall, CA: Carl Boyer, 3rd, 1977.

Glazier, I. A., ed. *The Famine Immigrants: Lists of Irish Immigrants Arriving at the Port of New York 1846–1851*. vols. 1–7. Baltimore: Genealogical Publishing Co., 1983.

Olsson, N. W. *Swedish Passenger Arrivals in New York 1820–1850*. Chicago: The Swedish Pioneer Historical Society, 1967.

Tepper, M., ed. *New World Immigrants*. vol. 1. Baltimore: Genealogical Publishing Co., 1979.

Tepper, M., ed. *Passengers to America*. Baltimore: Genealogical Publishing Co., 1977.

The Magazine of American Genealogy. *Immigrants to America Before 1750*. Chicago: The Institute of American Genealogy, 1929.

Whyte, D. *A Dictionary of Scottish Emigrants to the U.S.A*. Baltimore: Magna Carta Book Co., 1972.

Mayflower

Kellogg, L. M., ed. *Mayflower Families Through Five Generations: Descendants of the Pilgrims who Landed at Plymouth, Mass. December 1620*. vols. 1,2,3. General Society of Mayflower Descendants, 1975.

Roberts, G. B. *Genealogies of Mayflower Families: From The New England Historical and Genealogical Register*. Baltimore: Genealogical Publishing Co., 1985.

Early Settlers

Noyes, S., C. T. Libby, and W. G. Davis. *Genealogical Dictionary of Maine and New Hampshire*. Portland, ME: Southworth-Anthoensen, 1928–1939.

Savage, J. *A Genealogical Dictionary of the First Settlers of New England, Showing Three Generations of Those Who Came Before May, 1692, on the Basis of Farmer's Register*. Baltimore: Genealogical Publishing Co, 1969.

Talcott, S. V. *Genealogical Notes of New York and New England Families*. Baltimore: Genealogical Publishing Co., 1973.

Titcomb, S. E. *Early New England People*. Boston: W. B. Clarke & Carruth, 1882.

Ethnic

Blockson, C. L., and R. Fry. *Black Genealogy*. Englewood Cliffs, NJ: Prentice-Hall, 1977.

Hamilton-Edwards, G. *In Search of Welsh Ancestry*. Baltimore: Genealogical Publishing Co., 1986.

Hamilton-Edwards, G. *In Search of Scottish Ancestry*. Baltimore: Genealogical Publishing Co., 1972.

Rottenberg, D. *Finding Our Fathers A Guidebook to Jewish Genealogy*. New York: Random House, 1977.

Smith, J. C., ed. *Ethnic Genealogy: A Research Guide*. Westport, CT: Greenwood, 1983.

Zubatsky, D. S., and I. M. Berent. *Jewish Genealogy: A Sourcebook of Family History and Genealogies*. New York: Garland, 1984.

Miscellaneous

Webster's New Collegiate Dictionary. Springfield, MA: G. C. Merriam, 1979.

"Genealogy Fever Strikes." *The Hartford Current* (Hartford, CT) 17 April, 1983: 10B.

"History of the United States." *Encyclopedia Britannica: Macropaedia*. vol. 18, 15th ed., 1984:946.

"History of the United States." *Encyclopedia Britannica: Micropaedia*. vol. X., 15th ed., 1984: 274.

Levine, H. *Vocabulary for the College-bound Student*. New York: Amsco School, 1972.

Levine, H. *Vocabulary for the High School Student*. New York: Amsco School, 1972.

McFarlan, D., ed. *1990 Guinness Book of World Records*. New York: Sterling, 1989: 15.

"Military Service Records in the National Archives of the United States." *Guide to Genealogical Research in the National Archives*. Washington DC: Government, 1986.

"Pilgrim Fathers." *Encyclopedia Britannica: Micropaedia*. vol. VII., 15th ed., 1984: 1006.

"She'll Give Birth to Her Own Grandchildren." *Democrat and Chronicle* (Rochester, NY) 8 April, 1987: 2A.

"She Gives Birth to Her Grandchildren." *Democrat and Chronicle* (Rochester, NY) 2 October, 1987: 2A.

Wallis, Claudia. "The New Origins of Life." *TIME*, Sept. 10, 1984: 46.

INDEX

NOTES